Praise for *The Weekly*
Coaching Conversation

"Brian Souza is an author after my own heart. Don't miss this outstanding story! Not only is *The Weekly Coaching Conversation* a great story, but Brian also knows that, as a leader, you are nothing without your people. I highly recommend you read this engaging story and let it inspire you to become a better leader."

—Ken Blanchard, Coauthor of *The One Minute Manager*® *and Great Leaders Grow*

"Prepare to be entertained, inspired, and educated on what it really takes to begin the transformational journey from acting like a manager to becoming a leader. To get the most out of your organization, your team, or even yourself, *The Weekly Coaching Conversation* is an absolute must-read."

—Richard J. Bakosh, Global Managing Director, Accenture

"*The Weekly Coaching Conversation* is great for the mind and the soul. Powerful coaching!"

—Marshall Goldsmith, Author of *MOJO and What Got You Here Won't Get You There*

"Management folklore has a new hero, Coach—a colorful and crusty veteran with tons to teach eager high-achievers. Brian Souza artfully brings Coach to life in *The Weekly Coaching Conversation*, a book grounded solidly in rigorous research and practical experience, and written in a highly memorable and inviting style. The fictional world of *The Weekly Coaching Conversation* is packed with real-world dilemmas, timeless lessons, and unforgettable turns-of-phrase. It's a highly enjoyable read, and one you'll find yourself returning to often. *The Weekly Coaching Conversation* is a winner."

—Jim Kouzes, Coauthor of *The Leadership Challenge*, Dean's Executive Fellow of Leadership, Leavey School of Business, Santa Clara University

"*The Weekly Coaching Conversation* is a great read and will become the definitive guide for aspiring leaders. If you want to take your team's performance to the next level, read this book."

—Mark Silverman, President, The Big Ten Network

"*The Weekly Coaching Conversation* is full of warm, wonderful wisdom with timeless lessons for leadership and personal success."

—Brian Tracy, Author, *How the Best Leaders Lead*

"*The Weekly Coaching Conversation* cleverly teaches one of the essential truths of leadership—that it is no longer about you! This book offers frontline managers a way to accelerate their journey while offering experienced leaders a nostalgic reminder of the day they learned this truth and the inspiration to take their game to the next level."

—Liz Wiseman, Author, *Multipliers: How the Best Leaders Make Everyone Smart*

"*The Weekly Coaching Conversation* is a powerful book with an important message for all managers. In addition to a great story, in this book Brian Souza also presents a wonderful framework that will teach managers how to have a weekly coaching conversation with their team. I highly recommend it!"

—Verne Harnish, CEO, Gazelles, and Founder, Entrepreneurs' Organization (EO)

"Brian Souza's new book *The Weekly Coaching Conversation* is destined to become a classic in the world of business leadership and the pursuit of maximizing human potential. It is an inviting, enchanting, and awe-inspiring parable. I highly recommend Brian's new masterpiece."

—Michael Lardon M.D., Author of *Finding Your Zone: Ten Core Lessons for Achieving Peak Performance in Life and Sports*

"I thoroughly enjoyed reading *The Weekly Coaching Conversation* and highly recommend it. Brian Souza is a wonderful storyteller with a powerful message. The ideas presented in this book are the foundations of long-term success and should be required reading for all managers and aspiring leaders."

—John Daut, Senior Vice President of Sales, NetJets

"If you want to learn what it takes to lead and succeed in today's highly competitive corporate environment, read *The Weekly Coaching Conversation.* While it's an engaging story that makes it a quick read, the leadership message is timeless!"

—Rick Jackson, Chief Marketing Officer, VMWare, Inc.

"*The Weekly Coaching Conversation* cleverly teaches one of the essential truths of leadership—that it is no longer about you! This book offers frontline managers a way to accelerate their journey while offering experienced leaders a nostalgic reminder of the day they learned this truth and the inspiration to take their game to the next level."

—Liz Wiseman, Author, *Multipliers: How the Best Leaders Make Everyone Smart*

"*The Weekly Coaching Conversation* is a powerful book with an important message for all managers. In addition to a great story, in this book Brian Souza also presents a wonderful framework that will teach managers how to have a weekly coaching conversation with their team. I highly recommend it!"

—Verne Harnish, CEO, Gazelles, and Founder, Entrepreneurs' Organization (EO)

"Brian Souza's new book *The Weekly Coaching Conversation* is destined to become a classic in the world of business leadership and the pursuit of maximizing human potential. It is an inviting, enchanting, and awe-inspiring parable. I highly recommend Brian's new masterpiece."

—Michael Lardon M.D., Author of *Finding Your Zone: Ten Core Lessons for Achieving Peak Performance in Life and Sports*

"I thoroughly enjoyed reading *The Weekly Coaching Conversation* and highly recommend it. Brian Souza is a wonderful storyteller with a powerful message. The ideas presented in this book are the foundations of long-term success and should be required reading for all managers and aspiring leaders."

—John Daut, Senior Vice President of Sales, NetJets

"If you want to learn what it takes to lead and succeed in today's highly competitive corporate environment, read *The Weekly Coaching Conversation*. While it's an engaging story that makes it a quick read, the leadership message is timeless!"

—Rick Jackson, Chief Marketing Officer, VMWare, Inc.

THE WEEKLY
Coaching
Conversation

A BUSINESS FABLE

about taking your game and your team

to the next level

THE WEEKLY
Coaching
Conversation

A BUSINESS FABLE

about taking your game and your team

to the next level

BRIAN SOUZA

EVOLVE

ISBN: 978-0-9847625-1-4 paperback
ISBN: 978-0-9847625-2-1 hardcover
ISBN: 978-0-9847625-3-8 ebook

Published by Evolve Publishing, Inc. www.evolvepublishing.com

10 9 8 7 6 5 4 3 2 1

Printed in the United States of America.

===================

*To my amazing wife for all her love,
support, and friendship over the years.
And to my two beautiful daughters for
reminding me what it's all about.*

===================

Contents

Introduction

Whether your team is in an office, on a field, in a classroom, or in your living room—have you ever thought they had more to give, but you weren't quite sure how to get it out of them? Have you ever wanted them to play up to their potential, but didn't quite know how to make it happen? Are you looking for that one new idea, that one simple strategy that will take your career and your team's performance to the next level? If so, I wrote this book for you.

Over the past decade that I've been studying high-performance individuals and organizations, I've had the opportunity to sit down with dozens of world-class leaders and look under the hood of a number of first-rate organizations. Ironically, while I was initially in pursuit of a new theory of organizational productivity, I accidentally stumbled upon something much more profound. A truth, so simple in its construct and yet so significant in its application, that it literally changed my life.

In analyzing highly effective leaders of highly productive organizations, I discovered that the fundamental difference was not necessarily their IQ, strategic vision, operational prowess, or even charismatic persona—though these are obviously important ingredients. The fundamental difference primarily came down to one thing: their approach. They didn't act like a manager; they acted like a coach.

Like coaches, world-class leaders understand that the only way to systematically improve individual performance is by giving constructive coaching and developmental feedback. In fact, countless studies have proven that there's a direct correlation between the quantity and the quality of coaching an individual receives and his or her level of performance improvement.

Relying on quarterly performance reviews is not nearly enough to move the needle. Relying on someone else to come in once a year and train your team won't get the job done. Coaching and developing your people is not an event. It's an ongoing process that should be inextricably tied to everything you do.

Without a doubt, learning how to facilitate a weekly coaching conversation is the single most important skill you must master in order to improve your team's performance and your organization's productivity.

What exactly does that mean? How does one go about facilitating a coaching conversation? Where's the strategy? What's the plan? In short, that's what this book is all about. But this book is also about something else: having fun!

Have you ever noticed how most business books have a tendency to lull you to sleep before you get the takeaway? Well, with this book I decided to try something different—something new. While I did my best to pack as many new insights, actionable takeaways, and nuggets of wisdom as I could into these pages, I wanted this book to be entertaining first, and educational second. I wanted you to actually *want* to read this book, not feel that you had to because it was a gift from your boss.

Knowing full well that the only thing worse than a boring business book is a bad fable, I decided that if I was going to tell a story, I wanted to tell a good story—no, a great story. You know, the kind that not only motivates the mind, but also inspires the heart. The kind that makes you laugh, makes you think, and maybe even makes you shed a tear or two in the end.

The story you're about to read is about that first step we must all take on our journey to becoming a leader. The plot is centered around how Brad, a sales manager, gets an impromptu Ivy League lesson in leadership from an old college football coach at a dive bar. After recently turning around one of the company's worst-performing divisions and being named "Sales Leader of the Year," Brad thinks he has all the answers. That is, until he meets Coach. With the business acumen of Jack Welch and the motivational intensity of Vince Lombardi, Coach is a bundle

4

of contradictions. At one moment he's jokingly ranting mild obscenities, and the next he's dispensing wisdom like the Dalai Lama. At times he can be as militant as a drill sergeant and others as mellow as a Rastafarian. Despite his many contradictions, one thing is certain: *Everybody* loves Coach. As you'll soon discover, Coach shares with Brad a new system that not only transforms his career, but ultimately ends up changing his life.

Regardless of your position, industry, or where you might fall on an org chart, if you want to become a world-class leader, you must realize that the only way you can reach your potential is to first help your team achieve theirs. It is my sincere hope that this book inspires you to take that first critical step on your journey to the top and become a coach. As you're about to learn, coaching is not merely something that you, as a manager, must do. A Coach is someone that you, as a leader, must become.

Brian Souza
San Diego, CA

Party Time

Brad Hutchinson was riding high as he made his way down Interstate 280. His destination was Halftime—a famous dive bar just down the street from Stanford University in the otherwise yuppified city of Palo Alto, California. Brad was raring to celebrate. Just a few hours earlier, he had been named Sales Leader of the Year by the executive vice president of worldwide sales for NPC—a *Fortune* 500 high-tech company—at the company's regional awards meeting. But this wasn't just any award. In a results-focused, sales-driven company like NPC, it was *the* award. In a couple of weeks, the company's CEO would present Brad with the award at the company's annual black tie gala. A strange vibe, however, had greeted the

EVP's surprise announcement. The applause had been polite but light, and whispered reactions combined to form a murmur across the room. There had even been a few initial gasps. For some reason everyone, especially those on Brad's team, had been shocked that *he* had been selected to receive such a highly coveted award. Everyone, that is, except Brad. As far as he was concerned, all anyone had to do was to look at his numbers to see that he had earned it. After all, he had managed to transform one of the company's worst-performing divisions into one of the best in only a year.

For Brad, the award was his crowning career achievement and served as proof that he could transcend his rather humble roots. His drive and determination to succeed were rooted in his upbringing in a working-class family that at times felt lucky to just have enough milk for their Cheerios, let alone a silver spoon to eat with. After working his way through school and earning his bachelor's degree, Brad landed a sales job and quickly rose through the ranks. Senior management soon took note of this rising sales star and put him on the management fast-track—which only seemed to increase his appetite for more money, a bigger title, and more prestige. And the more he raced through life, the more he did it with a singular focus: himself. With that focus, however, came blind spots that would only become apparent in his new role as a frontline manager.

After the regional meeting had ended, Brad had invited his team to come help him celebrate at Halftime for Friday afternoon Happy Hour. Now as he sped down Interstate 280—swerving in and out of traffic, blaring the Black Eyed Peas through his stereo, singing "I Gotta Feeling" at the top of his lungs—he couldn't help but think, *Tonight's gonna be a good night.* He thought for sure that *this* night would be one of those legendary nights people would talk about and relive for years to come.

In a way, he was right.

Hero to Zero

Brad hit the scene at Halftime at 5:15 P.M., bursting through the doors with enough swagger to make Donald Trump seem like an introvert. With neon beer signs plastered on the walls, peanut shells scattered about the concrete floor, and a mishmash of old dartboards, oversized TVs, and undersized pool tables, Halftime was one of those unique watering holes where an eclectic mix of bar regulars, high-powered business executives, and university students came together to let their hair down and blow off steam.

Brad bellied up to bar and ordered a pint from Little Nikki. An imposing figure at 6' 5" with long black hair that flowed over his old, cutoff T-shirt and bulging biceps, Nikki looked more like the leader of the Hells Angels biker gang rather than the affable owner of one of the friendliest hangouts in town.

Brad shucked a few peanuts, throwing the shells on the floor as Nikki slid him a cold draft. He downed it like ice cold water on a hot summer day. He was there to celebrate, and tonight he planned to go *big*. So he ordered another and managed to polish it off as quickly as the first. With two pints down in less than 20 minutes, he figured he had better hit the head before the others showed up and the *real* party started.

As he made his way to the restroom toward the back of the bar, the Black Eyed Peas song still stuck in his head, and he thought to himself, *Yes, indeed . . . tonight's going to be a good night.*

Brad stood over the old tin horse trough, looking over last week's sports section pinned to the cork-board in front of him. Without warning, the door behind him flew open and crashed against the wall.

"That's an awful fancy suit you got on there!" bellowed a gruff voice. "Don't you think you're a little overdressed for a sh—hole like this? What—you just come from a funeral or somethin'?" said the voice with a laugh.

The young manager twisted his head as best he could, given the rather peculiar circumstances, and tried to get a look at the man behind the booming voice. He was surprised—and relieved—to see it wasn't one of the rougher-looking regulars he'd seen at the bar pounding shots of JD at five o'clock in the afternoon. This man was older—probably in his early 70s. He was smartly dressed and rather distinguished looking. It wasn't just the way he dressed that told the sales manager that this man was clearly very successful. It was also the way he carried himself: his presence. There was an aura about him that instantly put Brad at ease.

"No, not exactly," Brad said as he loosened his tie. "This isn't my usual Friday night getup. I actually just came from my region's annual awards meeting. I'm here to—"

"Awards meeting!" the old man interrupted in a loud but friendly tone. "Did you win anything?"

"Yep," Brad boasted, feeling more relaxed now that he'd finished his personal business. "I had a *huge* year. I absolutely crushed my number. In fact, just a few hours ago my EVP announced that I've been selected as the company's Sales Leader of the Year. And to top it off, this is only my first year as a manager!"

The old man went over to wash his hands as Brad, half-joking, added, "I guess this management stuff isn't so tough after all."

"I don't know about that," the old man said as they left the restroom and walked toward the bar together, "but Sales Leader of the Year in your first year as a manager? That's pretty darn impressive, kid. Congrats! So I take it you're here to celebrate?"

Brad glanced at his watch. "Yeah. In fact, my direct reports should be here any minute now. And don't be surprised if you see me riding that electric bull over there in a few hours. I have a feeling tonight's going to be one of *those* nights."

"Then let me be the first to buy you a celebratory cold one," the old man said as he motioned to Little Nikki for another round.

Brad thanked him for the pint and kept the friendly banter going.

"So what brings an old fart like you to a dive bar like this?" Brad joked, motioning with his head to a few bikers sitting at the bar. "You don't exactly look like you're with *those* guys."

The old man smiled. "Who? Old Thrasher? Don't worry. He may look tough, but he's one of the nicest guys you'll ever meet."

He continued, "I'm traveling a lot these days, so on Fridays whenever I'm in town I like to come down here to meet up with a few old friends to throw back a few, tell some lies, and reminisce about the good old days. You know how it is."

No sooner had the old man mentioned his buddies than one of them yelled at him from across the room.

"Hey, Coach!" his buddy called. "You gonna shoot pool or keep trying your tired pickup lines on the new guy?"

The group hanging out by the pool tables roared with laughter and exchanged high fives. The old man just shook his head and grinned.

"Listen," he said, grabbing his pint, "I'd better get back to my pool game before those sorry SOBs start trying to cheat. They know that's the only way they'll stand a chance. I'm like Minnesota Fats—I'm just too darn good!" He held up his glass for a toast and added, "Here's to you, kid. Sales Leader of the Year in your first year out of the gate? That's one hell of an accomplishment."

Back on his stool at the bar, Brad glanced at his watch. He thought for sure he had told the team to meet him at 5:30, but here it was 5:45 and no one had shown up yet. *No worries,* he thought, trying to reassure himself. *They'll show. After all, it is Friday at rush hour; they're probably just stuck in traffic or something.* He grabbed his phone and fired out a few text reminders.

Every time the front door swung open, Brad eagerly turned his head, expecting to see one of his team members. But the minutes ticked by and not one of them showed up. *Maybe they got lost,* he thought. So he grabbed his phone again and e-mailed them another reminder, this time with directions attached.

Meanwhile, he couldn't help noticing the constant flow of professionally dressed, middle-aged men and women streaming through the doors and making a beeline to the back of the bar where the old man he'd met earlier was holding court. Each one greeted the guy with an enthusiastic "Coach!" and accepted his bear hug as if they were long-lost friends.

Who is this guy? Brad wondered.

By 6:15, with no messages and no direct reports to be found, Brad began wondering if they were going to show up. *Of course they will,* he thought, desperately trying to convince himself. *Why wouldn't they?* Still, he decided he had waited long enough. It was time to kick things up a notch and really get the party started. He ordered another pint, but this time backed it up with a Purple Hooter.

A few more minutes passed. He checked his phone—still no messages. He glanced at the door—still no direct reports. He ordered another pint, another Purple Hooter, and a plate of nachos. Still no messages. Still no direct reports. Another pint, another Purple Hooter, and a plate of wings. Still no messages. Still no direct reports.

After an entire evening at the bar celebrating alone, the harsh reality finally sank in: *They're not going to show.*

Brad's heart sank. *I don't get it,* he thought. *Why didn't they come?* As if to add insult to injury, he couldn't help but look to the back of the room where at least a couple dozen people had now gathered around the old man, back-slapping, belly-laughing, and having a grand old time.

Meanwhile, back up at the bar all alone, dazed and confused, Brad was an emotional wreck. His stomach churned and he felt an aching emptiness inside. *How could one of the best nights of my life turn into one of the worst?* he wondered. *Didn't they understand the significance of this award? Didn't they appreciate the deals he had closed for them? What was wrong with them?*

Then it hit him: Had *he* done something wrong?

For the first time in a long time, Brad felt his once impenetrable shield of self-confidence crumble. At 9:00 P.M., he closed out his tab and headed to the restroom for a final pit stop before counting his losses and calling it a night.

Growing Pains

The old man deftly banked the nine ball off a side rail and into the far corner pocket and did a victory dance around the table to the hoots of the half dozen or so friends who remained with him in the back room of Halftime. The soiree had finally started to die down a bit, but those hanging around were still going strong.

Unbeknownst to Brad, the old man had been keeping an eye on him throughout the evening. Following his celebratory dance, he looked across the room and noticed Brad closing out his tab and heading toward the restroom. After handing his cue to one of the women in his group, he followed Brad to the men's room.

"Hey, kid" he jokingly hollered as he burst through the doors. "What happened to all those direct reports of yours? You didn't fire them, did ya?"

Brad lifted his face from the sink where he'd been splashing water in his eyes, partly in an attempt to sober up and partly in hopes that it might wake him from the horrible nightmare he was having.

"Oh, no big deal," he said. "You know how it is. I'm sure they had a good excuse. No worries."

The words rang hollow in the old man's ears. In the span of just a few hours, he'd watched as the once seemingly invincible young man had degenerated into a shell of his former self. Feeling compassion for the young manager, the old man decided to help him.

"Hey, kid" he said softly. "Just out of curiosity, would you mind if I ask you a question?"

"Sure," Brad said. "What's that?"

"When we were talking earlier, you said that you crushed *your* number, right? Well, my question is . . . how many people on your team crushed *theirs*?"

With that, the old man abruptly turned and walked away. Brad lifted his head from the sink and stared into the mirror, his face still dripping wet.

"What was *that* all about?" he said out loud. He reached for a paper towel, dried his face, and exited the restroom.

"Hey, wait a minute," he yelled in the old man's direction. "What are you talking about?"

The old man was walking slowly back toward the pool tables, as if to give Brad some time to ponder the depths of the question he had just asked. He turned back to Brad.

"Well, you said that your 'direct reports'—I believe is how you phrased it—were supposed to come here tonight to help *you* celebrate, because *you* crushed *your* number, right?"

"That's right," Brad replied. "What about it?"

"And they didn't show up, did they?"

"No, they didn't."

"So I was just curious if *they* had a reason to celebrate," the old man said.

The question hung in the air until the old man finally continued.

"How many 'direct reports' did you say you had again?" he asked.

"Ten," Brad said.

"And just out of curiosity, how many of *them* made *their* number?"

Brad paused a moment to think it over. "Five," he said. "And they wouldn't have even made their numbers if it hadn't been for *me* parachuting in at the bottom of the ninth inning to close a few monster deals for them."

"Ahhhhh," the old man said. "Now I see."

"See what?"

"So that's the reason they didn't show," the old man said under his breath. He looked back at the young manager and asked, "So how long have you had it?"

"Had what?" Brad asked, surprised by such a random question.

"A.A.M. Syndrome," the old man said without missing a beat.

"A.A.M. Syndrome?"

The old man's mischievous smile helped Brad relax just a little, but the next words from his mouth dealt a clean blow to Brad's ego.

"It's called 'All About Me Syndrome.' It's very common among frontline managers—*especially* sales managers. It's a frightening disease that causes its victims' heads to swell to twice their normal size, making them think they're a hell of a lot smarter than they actually are. It's brutal. I bet it's killed more careers than the Great Depression ever did!"

The old man could hardly contain his laughter. Brad, on the other hand, was clearly not amused.

"Ha, ha, old man," he said. "Very funny . . . now I get it."

"Do you? Do you really get it?" the old man said, cranking the intensity up a notch. "Tell you what. Since you think you've got all this management stuff figured out, let me ask you another question to see just how much you get it."

Brad stood silently, waiting. The old man appeared to be carefully choosing his next words.

"What's your job?" he finally asked.

The simplicity of the question disappointed Brad. Suddenly he wondered why he was even bothering with this conversation.

"What do you mean?" he snapped. "Like I told you, I'm a sales manager."

"Okay," the old man said, visibly struggling to maintain his composure. "In your role as a sales manager, what is your job?"

"Isn't that obvious?" Brad said flippantly. "To make my number."

Having had enough of the sales manager's pompous attitude, the old man lunged forward like a predator pouncing on prey.

"Wrong!" he said, nearly shouting. "Your job is not to make *your* number; it's to help your team members make *their* number."

Noticing that heads were starting to turn, the old man lowered his voice but didn't let up on his intensity.

"You're wondering why your direct reports didn't show up to help *you* celebrate?" he said. "It's because *they* don't have a reason to celebrate. Half of your team failed to achieve their goal. And for the other half that did, you said yourself that it was basically handed to them. There's no cause for celebration in failing. There's no joy in celebrating an empty victory that was handed to you."

Brad stood in silence, stunned.

"Kid, you just don't get it, do you?" the old man said. "In your new role, it's not about you anymore; it's about *them*. It's about *their* dreams, *their* goals, and *their* victories—not *yours*. And until you get that, you'll be just another typical manager who's in it to win it for himself."

"You know what your problem is?" the old man added. "You still think it's your job to be the smartest person in the room. It's not. In your new role, your job is to make everyone else on your team feel as if they're the smartest people in the room."

"What are you talking about?" Brad said in a slightly defensive tone. "I'm not supposed to be smart? I'm not supposed to make my number? Really?"

The old man sighed, unable to conceal his mounting frustration.

"Listen, kid," he said. "Over the years I've seen dozens of rookie managers just like you come through those doors in their knockoff suits and cheap Italian shoes, walking with a swagger they have yet to earn—thinking they have all the answers. The truth is, kid, you don't know squat. You may be a frontline *manager*, but you don't have the slightest clue about what it takes to become a frontline *leader*."

With that, the old man turned and started back toward his buddies by the pool table.

Another Disciple

Brad felt like a boxer barely able to get up from the floor after a series of brutal body blows. He may have been down, but he wasn't out. He decided to make one last attempt to salvage what little pride he had left.

"Hey, hold on a minute," he said. "I won Sales Leader of the Year, didn't I?"

The old man stopped and turned to look Brad dead in the eye.

"Kid, I hate to burst your bubble, but for you to lead, people must willingly follow. The fact that your team didn't show up tonight to help you celebrate speaks a hell of a lot louder than any trophy you may place on your mantel."

Brad's heart sank, not just because of what happened that evening or what the old man said, but because of *how* the old man said it. He remembered how lighthearted and fun-loving the old man was earlier in the evening, and it was obvious that he'd managed to really upset him. Brad knew that the guy was just trying to help. He started feeling something he hadn't experienced in years—remorse. He also knew something else: The old man was right.

Brad took a deep breath and said, "Hey listen, I want to apologize if I offended you. It's obviously been a pretty rough night for me."

With his emotions running high and plenty of liquid courage running through his veins, Brad decided to let down his guard, stop pretending, and for the first time just open up and acknowledge the truth.

"The truth is . . . the truth is . . ." He took another deep breath and quickly glanced around to make sure no one was within an earshot. "The truth is you're right. I don't have a friggin' clue about how to be a frontline manager, let alone a frontline leader. You want to know why I parachute in to close big deals for my reps? It's because that's all I've been trained to do. I'm a sales guy. When I was promoted, I was basically thrown out there without any coaching and told to sink or swim. I'm not sinking, but I'm sure as hell not doing synchronized swimming, either."

"Really?" the old man said, lifting an eyebrow and cracking a smile. "I think you'd look pretty cute in one of those outfits with your hair all up in a bun."

They both had a good laugh, which helped diffuse the tension in the air.

The raw honesty and humility in Brad's response struck a chord with the old man. He wondered if the combination of his Irish temper and the Irish whiskey hadn't gotten the better of him. He decided he'd been too hard on the young manager, especially given all that the kid had been through that evening.

The old man had been officially retired for quite some time, and it had been years since he'd taken on a new protégé. He took a minute to consider whether or not he had the time and energy to help this young man, given his other charitable and business interests. Finally, the look of confusion and desperation in the young manager's eyes convinced him that he had to get involved. Although the kid hadn't openly asked for any help, the old man felt compelled to at least offer.

"I like you, kid, so here's the deal," he said. "You seem like you've got some talent, some humility, and a lot of fire. And that's a rare combination these days. If you're up for it—if you really want to learn how to become a frontline leader—I can help. But only under one condition."

"What's that?"

"I want you to promise that you'll pay it forward."

"Pay it forward?"

"I want you to promise me that you'll use what I'm about to teach you to make a positive difference in people's lives. I'll invest in you as long as you promise to invest in others."

Brad took a deep breath. Sure, he barely knew this guy. But he was definitely in need of some serious help, and he had a hunch that the old man could provide it. So he decided to follow his gut instinct.

"Done," Brad said.

With a smile the old man extended his hand. "Mick Donnelly," he said, "but you can call me 'Coach.'"

"Brad Hutchinson," Brad said as he shook Mick's hand, "but you can call me 'Sales Manager.'"

Coach smiled, patted Brad's back, and said, "Now go home and get some rest. I'll meet you right back here next Friday at 5:30. And don't be late."

As they parted ways, Coach turned and called, "Oh, and one more thing. I want you to do a little homework over the next week."

Homework? Brad thought to himself. But he wasn't about to question his new coach before they even got started.

"Sure," Brad said, "what's that?"

"I want you to chew on this question: Why is it that the best players often make the worst coaches?"

Brad gave him a thumbs-up and headed out the door to hail a cab.

Coach's Secret

Brad spent his weekend mentally going over his encounter with Coach and wondering what he'd gotten himself into by agreeing to meet with this mysterious character. But he also felt relief, sensing that this outspoken gentleman was about to help him conquer some management challenges he didn't even know existed. At work that week Brad—unsure of how to handle the situation of his team's not showing up—pretended as if nothing had happened.

The following Friday he arrived at Halftime 15 minutes early, vaguely remembering Coach saying something about not being late. He grabbed a stool at the bar next to a man in his mid-50s who was sporting designer jeans and a sharp-looking sports coat. The man casually looked in Brad's direction—then did a double take.

"Hey, aren't you that guy that Coach was talking to last week?" he asked.

Brad, always good with names and faces, quickly placed this one.

"I am, indeed," he said. "And I believe you were shooting pool with the guy who made the joke about Coach using his pickup line on me."

The man grinned and nodded.

"I have to admit, that was pretty damn funny," Brad added.

"I'm Randy Johnson," the man said, extending his hand. "But since you're with Coach, you can call me R.J."

Brad returned the favor. "I'm Brad Hutchinson," he said with a smile. "But since you're friends with Coach, you can call me Sales Manager." Brad slid a bowl of peanuts between them and cracked one open. "So, R.J, how do you know Coach?" he asked.

"Gosh, we've probably been friends for more than 20 years now," he responded. "I was actually on his team years ago when we worked for a small start-up company together."

Brad recalled that RJ and Coach had interacted more like long-lost college buddies than former co-workers. "You used to *work* for him?" he said with surprise. "So who were all those other people in the group? Was it someone's birthday or something?"

"Well, we like to say that we're all a part of Coach's crew. At some point in our careers, we've all been fortunate enough—blessed, really—to have worked for Coach. Whenever he's in town, we all like to spend time with him and thank him for all he's done for us and our careers over the years."

Brad couldn't hide the shock on his face. "But there must have been 30 people back there!"

"And there's probably hundreds—maybe even thousands—more around the world," RJ said. "Coach has touched a lot of lives over the years, both directly and indirectly. He's an amazing human being and by far the best boss I've ever had. I've learned more from Coach about what it takes to lead and succeed in a few Happy Hour sessions sitting right back there in

Coach's corner than I did earning my MBA. And trust me, feeding Coach a couple of pints is a hell of a lot cheaper than my tuition was!"

RJ took a sip from his pint and asked, "So what about you? How long have you known Coach?"

"Actually, I just met him for the first time last Friday," Brad said. "To make a *very* long story short, it became pretty obvious that night that I have some serious management challenges with my team that I didn't even know I had. I guess the old man felt sorry for me and volunteered to help me out. In fact," Brad said as he looked down at his watch, "he should be here any minute now."

"Consider yourself a very lucky man," RJ said with enthusiasm. "If I were you, I'd absorb every word that comes out of his mouth. He paused for a moment, considering Coach's penchant for profanity. "Well, almost every word," he added with a chuckle. "If it weren't for him, I'd probably still be stuck in the same frontline manager role I was in when he found me!"

"What do you do now?" Brad asked.

"Who me? Oh, I'm in marketing."

RJ showed no desire to expand on his resume, so Brad shifted the conversation back to Coach.

"I can't get over the fact that all those people who worked for Coach so long ago still worship the ground he walks on and want to hang out with him," Brad said. "That's unbelievable. I can't even get my team to share a pint with me, and I'm still their damn boss!" Brad cracked open another peanut and tossed it in his mouth. "So what's his secret?"

"That's the funny part," RJ said. "You'd think he was some type of management guru or academic scholar or something. He's not. In fact, I don't think he even went to business school. I think he studied sports psychology or some damn thing."

RJ paused, looking thoughtful as he sipped his drink. "His secret is all in his approach," he continued. "He's not a manager; he's a coach."

"A coach?"

"Yeah, believe it or not, he actually played a couple years of pro football back in the day. But after that didn't pan out, he started coaching college football and eventually became the head coach for a small

The secret is all in the approach. Stop acting like a manager and starting acting like a coach.

Ivy League school. After a couple of rough seasons, the long hours and stress began taking its toll on his health and he was forced to quit."

"Wow, that's crazy. So how did he end up in the business world?" Brad asked.

But before RJ could answer, the front door to the bar swung open.

"Coach!" everyone in the bar yelled in unison.

"Well, speak of the devil," said RJ. "I'd better let *him* finish the story."

The Moment

Coach made the rounds as he strolled into Halftime, greeting everyone with high-fives and hugs as if it had been months, not one week, since he'd last seen them. He eventually made his way over to RJ, put him in a headlock, and hollered, "RJ, you sorry SOB! You aren't telling lies about me again are you?"

"Come on, Coach, you know me better than that," he said, and then added, "Of course I am!"

Coach laughed. "Yeah, just remember you still owe me five bucks for that whippin' I gave you shootin' pool the other night," he said. "And I don't want to hear any excuses. Now that you're a big-time CMO, you shouldn't have any problem coming up with the cash."

He looked over at Brad.

"Sales Manager! How the hell are ya?" Coach said. "Looks like you finally recovered from all those Purple Tweeters you were drinking last Friday. That's sure some pretty hard stuff, isn't it? It'll knock you on your a— if you're not careful!"

Brad laughed, along with everyone else in the bar.

"No kidding," Brad said. "I noticed Thrasher drinking all the JD so I figured a Purple Hooter was the next best thing."

Thrasher cast a quizzical look in Brad's direction. He could barely remember where he was last Friday, let alone who this young punk was that somehow knew his name.

With the universal "I need two pints" hand signal, Coach motioned to the far side of the bar where Little Nikki was clearing away some empty glasses. "Comin' your way, Coach," he said.

When their pints arrived, Brad and Coach made their way back to the far corner of the bar, where the young manager noticed a normal-looking booth with a four-inch-tall bronze plate on the front wall that read "Coach's Corner." On the back wall hung a giant chalkboard, and the side walls were pinned with dozens of celebratory pictures of Coach and his crew that had been taken at Halftime over the years.

"Take a seat, Sales Manager," Coach said as he slid into the booth. "So . . . pretty interesting week last week, huh?"

"Yeah, it was pretty rough on a lot of levels," Brad replied.

"Did you have a chance to noodle on some of the things we talked about?"

"I did, and let's just say I didn't get a whole lot of sleep," Brad said. "I kept thinking about what you said—that I was acting just like every other typical manager who's in it to win it for himself, and that I didn't have the slightest clue about what it took to become a frontline leader."

"And?" Coach prompted.

"It's true," Brad said. "But I don't want to be just like every other frontline manager. I want to become a frontline *leader*. The problem is, I don't even know what the heck that means, let alone know how to become one."

Coach tossed a peanut about four feet into the air and caught it effortlessly in his mouth when it came down.

"Look, kid, I hate to break it to you, but you ain't gonna become Winston Churchill overnight. Becoming a leader is a process that takes time. And given that we only have a couple weeks together, we have one goal and one goal only: to teach you the single most important thing you need to know about, so that when your leadership moment finally arrives, you're ready for it."

"Leadership moment?"

"Make a note," Coach said. "One of the keys to succeeding in life is to be ready when your time comes. Everything you do, everything you learn, and everything you experience is all preparing you for that one critical moment. I call it the leadership moment. Think of it as a rite of passage that all great leaders must go through. Washington had his at Valley Forge; Gandhi had his on the Salt March; Rosa Parks had hers on a bus; and Mother Teresa had hers on the streets of Calcutta. It's that split second in time when one's preparedness is challenged, one's character is

tested, and one's destiny is determined. It's the very first time when people follow you—not because they *have to,* but because they *want to.*"

Brad reached into his pocket for a pen, but he had nothing to write on.

Coach, who'd apparently anticipated this moment, pulled out a new pocket-sized journal and handed it to Brad.

"I don't have many rules, but here's one non-negotiable: Never come to one of my coaching sessions without this journal," he said. "In fact, don't go anywhere without it. I always have mine with me 24/7." He pulled a tattered-looking journal from his pocket and held it up.

Brad took his new journal and jotted down some notes as Coach moved on to the most random question he'd asked yet.

"Do you like the French?" he asked.

Brad stammered, unsure of how to answer such a bizarre question. "Well, I . . ."

"Me either," Coach quipped without missing a beat as he tossed another peanut in the air. "But there's one Frenchman I do respect, and that's Napoleon—not because of his morals or values, but because of what he achieved at such an early age. Did you know that Napoleon became a general at 24, ruler of France at 33, and emperor at only 35?

Do you want to know how he did it?"

"Let me see, if memory serves me, by having short-man's disease and slaughtering a lot of people."

Coach laughed, but kept on point.

"There was one transformational event—a leadership moment—early in his career during the Battle of Toulon that changed everything for Napoleon. That singular event not only changed how everyone else saw Napoleon; more important, it changed how Napoleon saw *himself*. For the first time, he didn't just *think* he had what it took to become a leader—he *knew* it."

Coach leaned forward in his seat, his eyes wide. "Napoleon's troops were outnumbered ten to one, and defeat appeared imminent. Napoleon realized he couldn't wait on orders from Paris, so he decided to step up and take charge. With rain pouring down, he mounted his horse, rode out in front of his troops, and shouted, 'Gentlemen, it looks like history has made room for us after all! If any of you don't feel like going, that's fine . . . I do! I'll take this fort alone and destiny will be waiting. . . . Bullets will bounce off me. . . . Cannon balls will swerve with fear. . . . Not one of you need take this fort, but I absolutely *insist* you come with me and watch *me* take it. . . . If I go forward, follow me. . . . If I retreat, shoot me. . . . If I am killed, avenge me!'

"With that, Napoleon led the charge. Toulon fell, saving the French Revolution and forever memorializing Napoleon's place in history."

Coach's horrible attempt at a French accent echoed throughout the bar as Brad cracked up with laughter.

"Ohhhhh . . . now I get it," Brad said. "You want me to start riding around my office on horseback wearing a silly little hat and yelling, 'Charge!'"

"Okay, smart a—, are you done?" Coach asked.

"Sorry, Coach," Brad said with a chuckle. "Couldn't resist."

"Seriously," Coach said. "I want you to absorb what I'm teaching you so that when your leadership moment arrives, you're prepared to seize it."

"How will I know when my leadership moment arrives?" Brad asked. "What if I miss it?"

"You'll know, trust me. The only question is—will you be ready? Will you step up and seize the moment to prove to yourself and everyone else that you have what it takes to become a leader? Or will you forever be relegated to the ranks of the myriad managers who fail to live up to their potential? Only time will tell, kid. But when that moment comes and it's just you standing on that stage—all alone in the spotlight—only you will have the power to make it happen."

Empty the Cup

Brad headed to restroom and was on his way back when RJ nearly bumped into him.

"Hey, champ," RJ said. "How's it going back there?"

"Great, I'm learning tons about the French Revolution," Brad said with a smile.

RJ laughed, having heard Coach's Napoleon story more times than he'd care to remember.

"Hey, I almost forgot to mention something," he said. "Be sure and ask Coach about the time he almost got fired from his first management job." As he walked away, he added in a loud voice, "Oh, and don't forget to ask him about the system!"

Brad walked back to the Coach's corner, but before he could even sit down, Coach said, "I saw you chatting with RJ. What was that all about?"

"I don't know, something about you almost getting canned from your first management job."

"Next to salespeople, marketing people have the biggest darn mouths, I tell you. I bet he told you all about my story, didn't he?"

Not wanting to throw his new friend under the bus, Brad responded, "He didn't go into too much detail. All he told me was that you used to be a college football coach and then you made the switch into business. But I'd love to hear more about it."

"All right," Coach said, glancing at his watch. "I guess I can at least give you a quick one-two on my background."

Coach explained that he'd grown up idolizing his father, a successful high school football coach, and how he'd always wanted to follow in his footsteps. After a successful playing career and a few years as an assistant, Coach landed his dream job: head coach at his Ivy League alma mater. But the university wasn't as committed to winning as he was, and as the losses started to pile up, the stress continued to mount. Eventually, his doctors recommended he find a different line of work before he suffered a serious heart attack.

"After I hung up my whistle and left the sidelines for good, I was devastated," Coach said. "I was already in my mid-thirties, and all I'd ever known was coaching. I had absolutely no idea what I was going to do next. Fortunately, an old college football teammate happened to be an executive for a communications firm in New York. Somehow he managed to help me land a job as a sales manager with his company."

"Really?" Brad said. "Did you have any sales experience?"

"Nope."

"Wow, that's crazy! How did you manage to pull it off?"

"I didn't, at first. In fact, my new management career was almost over before it even began. After about six months it became apparent to everyone—especially my team—that I had absolutely no idea what the hell I was doing."

"So what did you do?"

"Panicked. That's when I started devouring every management book I could find. You name it, I read it. But for some reason, the more management gimmicks I tried, the worse things got. Finally, one day I'd had enough. I walked up to my buddy's office and told him I was going to quit."

"Are you serious?" Brad said. "What did he say?"

"He looked me in the eyes and said something that completely changed my life. He said, 'Listen, Mick. I didn't stick my neck on the line for you because I thought you'd make a good *manager*. I stuck my neck on the line for you because I knew you'd make a great *coach*. So do us both a favor. Stop acting like a *manager* and start acting like a *coach*.' And boom! Just like that, it hit me. I made a decision then and there to start coaching my team in the office the same way I used to coach my team on the field."

"What an amazing story," Brad said. "So is this where the secret system RJ was telling me about comes in?"

"Easy, big shooter," Coach said. "One step at a time. Let's not get ahead of ourselves. I believe you had some homework to do. Did you do it?"

"Yep."

"Okay, so what are your thoughts?" Coach said.

"First off, I guess I'm a little confused," Brad said. "The other night I came in here feeling pretty good about myself—like I had all this management stuff all figured out. But after my team stood me up and you put me in my place, I guess I left with a lot more questions than answers."

Coach chuckled and nodded in approval. "Make a note," he said. "As a leader, your job is not to have all the right answers; it's to ask all the right questions. Speaking of which, have you heard about the scholar who traveled to Tibet to discuss Buddhism with a wise old monk?"

By now Brad was getting used to Coach's rather unique coaching style, so he simply said, "No," without even looking up from his notebook.

"As soon as the scholar arrived at the monastery," Coach continued, "the monk invited him inside to have a cup of tea. While the monk prepared the tea, the scholar began spewing all that he had learned about Buddhism while studying at the university. On and on he kept rambling, trying to impress the monk with how much he knew about Buddhism. Meanwhile, the wise old monk just quietly listened as he prepared the tea. When the tea was finally ready, the monk began to pour it into the scholar's cup as the scholar continued lecturing. And he continued pouring the tea, even though the scholar's cup was already overflowing. When the hot tea ran off the table and onto the scholar's leg, he jumped out of the chair and shouted, 'You old fool! What are you thinking?' The old monk calmly replied, 'A cup that is already full has no room to receive.'"

Coach reached for a handful of peanuts.

"I'm not following you," said Brad with a puzzled look. "My homework was to think about why the best players often make the worst coaches. Is there some sort of connection here?"

"There is," said Coach. "The best players often fail to make the leap from player to coach because they fail to empty the cup. Think about it. Michael Jordan, the greatest basketball player who ever stepped on a court, failed miserably as head of basketball operations for the Washington Wizards. Wayne 'The Great One' Gretzky spent four years as head coach of the Phoenix Coyotes and failed to make the playoffs even once. Ted Williams, Magic Johnson—the list goes on and on."

"I think I see what you're saying," Brad said. "When they transitioned from their role as an individual contributor into the role of a coach, they thought they had it all figured out. Their cup was full, so to speak."

"Exactly," Coach said. "Along those lines, here's another little nugget you may want to jot down: To succeed at the next level, you've got to realize that the rules of the game have changed—and so too must you. If you really want to transform yourself from a manager into a leader, you're going to need a new approach—a new playbook, if you will. You're going to need a system to get the most out of your team on a consistent basis."

The first step to becoming a frontline leader is to realize that the rules of the game have changed—and so too, must you.

"All right, already!" Brad blurted. "What's this secret system I keep hearing about?"

Coach took a quick look around. In a voice slightly above a whisper, he raised his eyebrows and said, "You really want to know, huh?"

Brad nodded with eager anticipation.

"Okay, so you know how they say patience is a virtue, right?"

Brad hung on every word uttered out of the old man's mouth, anticipating something truly profound.

"Well, why don't you be a virtuous young lad and get this old fart another pint while I sit here waiting patiently."

Coach roared with laughter, and Brad just shook his head as he begrudgingly made his way back up to the bar.

The System

While Brad was at the bar waiting for another round of drinks, Coach was busy jotting down questions on the back of an old flyer that had been pinned to the wall. Then he grabbed a cocktail napkin and sketched out a simple chart composed of four squares. When Brad returned with their drinks, Coach pulled a sheet of paper from his tattered journal.

"Here," Coach said, handing the paper to Brad. The noise level in the bar had grown louder as the Friday Happy Hour got rolling, so Coach raised his voice against the commotion. "I want you to answer these questions."

Brad scanned the sheet, noticing ten questions along the lines of *On a scale from 1–10, how confident are you that your team trusts you and believes that you have their best interests in mind?*

Brad looked up from the paper. "These are some interesting questions, but I don't see how this has anything to do with me doing my job and making my number," he said somewhat defensively.

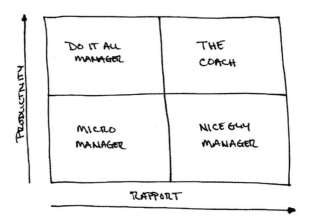

MANAGEMENT APPROACH MATRIX

"Trust me," Coach said. "This has *everything* to do with you making your number."

Brad quickly plowed through the list, answering the questions. He handed the sheet back to Coach.

Staring intently through the reading glasses on the tip of his nose, pen in hand, Coach looked like a university professor grading a student's pop quiz. Using the sketch he'd drawn on the napkin, he tallied Brad's responses by making a mark next to one of the four squares, depending on how Brad had answered each question. Brad watched and wondered until finally Coach took off his reading glasses and looked up.

"Yep, I knew it," Coach said, exhaling loudly. "You're a classic Do-It-All Manager."

Brad was at once curious and defensive.

"Do-It-All Manager?" he said.

Coach calmly slid the napkin his way.

"I've been coaching managers and developing leaders since long before you were even a twinkle in your mother's eye," he said. "And if there's one thing I've learned, it's that there are basically only four types of managers. Just by asking a handful of targeted questions, I can pinpoint a manager's approach in only a few minutes. Want to know what's even more interesting?"

"Sure, what's that?"

"If you ask the frontline manager's team the same set of questions, nine times out of ten there's a huge disconnect between how well the managers think their doing and how well their *team* thinks their doing. The sad part is, most managers are completely oblivious to the fact that their approach is causing harm to their relationship with their team and paralyzing their productivity."

Coach tapped his finger on the four-square matrix, his eyes fixed on Brad.

"Each type of manager has a very distinctive style or approach. Let me give you a few quick examples. First, when you think of the term *micromanager*, what immediately comes to mind?"

"I think of that annoying boss in the movie *Office Space*," Brad said without even thinking about it. "You know, the guy with the huge glasses and the obnoxious suspenders that keeps bugging Peter about putting a cover sheet on his TPS report."

The look on Coach's face indicated he'd obviously never seen the movie.

"Okay, well anyway," Brad went on. "I think of someone who's anal . . . always right . . . you know, always in your business."

"That's right," Coach said. "A micromanager cares more about making sure his people do things perfectly than he does about helping them improve their performance. Micromanagers are typically perceived as being distrustful, controlling, uncaring, and bossy, right? So let me ask you: How do you think this particular management approach makes the people on his team *feel?*"

"I guess it makes them feel stressed out . . . resentful . . . unmotivated . . . and unhappy."

"And how does coming to work every day feeling stressed out, resentful, unmotivated, and unhappy impact his team's morale and their level of productivity?" Coach asked.

"Not in a good way," Brad said.

"Exactly," Coach said. "The micromanager's approach causes his team to put forth just enough effort to skate by—to fly below the radar in hopes of collecting another paycheck."

Coach then pointed to the box in the bottom left corner labeled "Micromanager."

"With this approach," he said, "is it any surprise that micromanagers typically have the lowest level of productivity and the worst rapport with their teams?"

"No," Brad agreed.

Coach turned his attention to the box in the lower right corner.

"So what comes to mind when you think of a Nice Guy Manager?" he asked.

"I think of someone who's laid back, mellow, hands off—maybe even at times a little disengaged," he said.

"Good. In general, Nice Guy Managers are more concerned with being liked by their team than they are with getting results from them," Coach said. "And when a manager's approach is *too* laid back or *too* hands off—how do you think that impacts the team's level of productivity?"

"I don't know, I guess the top 10 percent probably do pretty well," Brad said, "but the bottom 90 percent who may need a little coaching probably suffer."

"You're learning, Sales Manager," Coach said. "Good work."

Then Coach turned his attention to the box in the upper left corner. With a smirk on his face, Coach said, "Now here's one that shouldn't be too hard for you to figure out: The Do-It-All Manager. How would you describe your—er, excuse me—this management approach?"

"Very funny," Brad said.

Coach waited for an answer, but Brad just sat there silently with his arms crossed.

"Look, kid," Coach said, "I'm not here to tell you what you *want* to hear; I'm here to tell you what you *need* to hear. Everything I'm teaching you is preparing you so that when your leadership moment comes, you can step up and make it happen—because you never know when, or if, you'll get another chance. So you can either listen and learn, or not. The choice is yours. . . . Shall I continue?"

Brad took a breath, uncrossed his arms, and nodded a bit sheepishly.

"Okay, then," Coach continued. "The Do-It-all Manager isn't a bad person. His priorities are just screwed up. He's selfish. As far as he's concerned, it's his world and everyone else is just livin' in it. As a result, he's often perceived as being arrogant, uncaring, distrustful, distant, cold, cocky—"

Brad cut him off. "All right, all right. Enough already. I get your point."

Coach, however, wanted to make sure the message really sank in.

"This is very important," he continued. "I want you to imagine that *this* is your reality. Forget about *your* perspective for a minute and put yourself in your team members' shoes. How do you think your arrogant, uncaring, cold management approach makes them feel?"

Brad resisted the urge to roll his eyes.

"I don't know," he said. "I guess it might make them feel a little frustrated and unmotivated."

Coach sat across the table and said nothing, purposely creating a long, awkward silence.

"And," Brad added after giving it some more thought, "I guess they might feel a little unappreciated . . . unimportant . . . maybe even a little sad."

Coach softened his tone. "And if your team comes to work feeling frustrated, unmotivated, unappreciated, unimportant, and maybe even a little sad," he said, "how might that impact their productivity, their motivation, their self-confidence, and their sense of self-worth? How might feeling that way 50 hours a week impact their families?"

Brad felt his eyes tearing up and looked away. When he returned his gaze to Coach, he pushed past the lump in his throat and answered the question.

"You know, I've never thought of it that way," he said, gazing into the distance as if he were talking to himself. "I've really never thought of it that way. . . ."

"You see, kid, it's not all about the numbers," Coach said. "In the short run, you may manage to put some points on the board and place some trophies on the mantle, but that's just because you're hogging the ball and stealing all the glory. I want you to always remember something, kid. When all is said and done and we've completed this journey we call life, what will matter most is not we have achieved—but rather who we have become."

When all is said and done and we've completed this journey we call life, what will matter most is not we have achieved—but rather who we have become.

A New Approach

One of the old man's friends, Linda Sweeny, approached Coach's corner, eyed the two men sitting at the table, and immediately sensed some tension.

"I hate to interrupt such a festive conversation," she blurted. "But I'd like to remind you that *some* people are here to have a good time."

Brad, still reeling from coming face-to-face with the reality of how his flawed management approach had adversely impacted his team, did his best to muster a smile.

Linda put her hand on Brad's shoulder.

"Don't feel bad," she said reassuringly. "All of us have been on the receiving end of this coaching conversation many times over the years. Coach may make

Jack Welch look like a pussycat at times, but I guarantee if you do what he says, it will not only improve your team's performance and your organization's productivity—it'll change your life."

"What the hell is this, an infomercial or somethin'?" Coach jokingly barked, cutting her off before her flattery made him even more uncomfortable. "Get back over there and start warming up those darts. I'll be over in a sec to give you a chance to redeem yourself."

As Linda left, Coach returned his attention to his protégé.

"Now where was I?" he said.

"I don't know," said Brad, "but I'm hoping you're going to tell me how to change my approach, because right about now I'm feeling like a pretty big jerk."

"Oh yeah, now I remember," Coach continued. "The typical frontline manager acts more like an individual contributor, while a frontline *leader* acts more like a coach. That's why we call him a coach."

Coach pointed to the upper right-hand quadrant on the napkin.

"As you see here," he said, "the Coach consistently achieves the highest level of productivity, while at the same time earning the highest level of trust and rapport with his team. I can assure you that this is no coincidence. The two go hand in hand."

"How so?" Brad asked.

"Make a note," Coach said. "Great coaches consistently get the most *out* of their people because they consistently put the most *into* their people. They believe in their people, want them to succeed, and are committed to coaching and developing them so that they consistently perform to the maximum of their ability."

Brad scribbled notes as fast as he could.

"Let me ask you a question," Coach said. "Hypothetically speaking, what if you stopped acting like a manager and started acting like a coach? How do you think this new approach might change the dynamics of the relationship with your team?"

Brad took a deep breath while he pondered the possibilities. "Well, for starters they'd probably feel more valued . . . trusted . . . appreciated . . . confident . . . and maybe even a little fired up to come into work."

Great coaches consistently get the most out of their people because they consistently put the most into their people.

"And what if you could create an environment—an organizational culture—where your people felt valued, trusted, appreciated, confident, and maybe even fired up to come into work?" Coach asked. "How might that impact their productivity? Better yet, how might that impact *your* productivity as a leader?"

Brad got the point, but he hesitated before responding. "I don't know, I guess I'm still having a tough time envisioning myself as a leader," he confessed. "I mean, when I think of leadership, I don't think of a lowly frontline manager like me way down in the trenches. I think of the bigwigs up in the ivory tower making all the strategic decisions."

"Listen, kid. When you've been around as long as I have, you'll realize that strategy ain't squat without execution. Let the big cheeses up in the ivory tower worry about crafting the organizational vision, strategy, and plan. As a frontline leader, it's your job to get bottom-up buy-in on that plan, execute the strategy, and transform that vision into reality."

"Easier said than done," Brad replied. "I must have told my team what to do a thousand times. They know what to do—they're just not doing it."

"Write this down," Coach said. "Leaders don't just tell their team what to do. A prison guard can do that. Leaders invest the time to understand their people's dreams and goals—then they align their team's personal interests with the interests of the company. Frontline leaders help bridge the gap between what the company wants and what their team wants, to make sure that everyone's rowing in the same direction."

Coach paused, thought for a moment, and then leaned forward for added emphasis.

"Before I forget, I want to make an important distinction that very few people understand," he said. "Coaching is not merely something that you, as a manager, must do. A Coach is someone that you, as a leader, must become."

"Wow, that's pretty profound stuff," Brad said. "The way you're describing this new management approach, it seems like a no-brainer. But if that's the case, then why are there so many bad managers out there?"

Coaching is not merely something that you, as a manager, must do. A Coach is someone that you, as a leader, must become.

"'They may be bad managers, but they're not bad people," Coach said. "And the reason most of them are bad managers isn't actually even their fault. They've never been trained on the single most important skill set they need to know—coaching. It's amazing. People wonder why most teams in most organizations are so dysfunctional. It's pretty simple: There's no coach! How can you expect managers to coach and develop their team when they haven't even received any coaching themselves?"

Brad nodded. "Good point. At least that makes me feel a *little* better."

Coach cracked open another peanut and waited patiently for the sales manager's next question.

"Okay, so let me ask you something else," Brad said. "Based on your experience, what would you say is the single most important thing I need to know about becoming a world-class leader or a coach?"

"Simple," Coach said without hesitation. "At its core, leadership isn't a head issue; it's a heart issue. Most managers today have it all wrong. They're so wrapped up in their damn spreadsheets, PowerPoint

slides, and Six Sigma BS that somewhere along the line they forgot these aren't machines we're dealing with—they're people. They don't realize that as a coach, the more you give, the more you'll get. The more you care, the more they'll contribute."

Coach paused to take a sip from his pint and then added, "If you want to become a coach, here's my advice: Get your heart right first and your head will follow."

Brad was furiously taking notes, trying to capture what he was hearing and process it so he could ask follow-up questions.

"Okay, I hear what you're saying, but if my role as a coach is to constantly evaluate, coach, and develop my team," he said, "don't tactics and strategies—or, as you put it, 'head issues'—play a pretty important part in that process?"

"Absolutely. Listen, I'm not saying that teaching your people the fundamentals isn't important. It is," Coach said. "It just shouldn't be your very first priority. That's because change cannot be imposed; it must be chosen. In order to get people to improve, they first have to *want* to improve."

As a coach the more you give, the more you'll get. The more you care, the more they'll contribute.

Coach pointed toward a nearby television tuned to a local news channel that was airing a piece on the San Francisco 49ers.

"When Bill Walsh took over as head coach of the 49ers back in '79," Coach began, "how did he transform the demoralized team with a 2–14 record that he inherited into the Super Bowl champs just 24 months later?"

"I don't know," Brad shot back, "but I'm guessing that drafting Joe Montana and Jerry Rice probably didn't hurt."

"Actually, Walsh won his first championship in '81 but didn't draft Rice until '85," Coach said. "But that's beside the point. When Walsh took over as head coach, his first priority wasn't teaching his players new schemes or even fussing over perfecting the fundamentals.

His first priority was to implement a new system, a new playbook—something he called his Standard of Performance. He knew he had to raise his team's standards of what they expected from themselves and each other. He got them to believe that with hard work and a commitment to excellence, they could become world champs."

"And he did it by—" prompted Brad.

"By constantly communicating the four most powerful words a leader can say: *I believe in you.*" Coach paused, but not long enough for the sales manager to pepper him with another question. "I want you to remember something: Behind every great player is a coach who believed in that player more than the player believed in himself."

Coach was on a roll now. As the young manager wrote his notes, he did his best to maintain some eye contact.

"Over the years," Coach went on, "I've coached some amazing people who have gone on to achieve some extraordinary things. And I see every bit as much potential in you as I did in them. But here's the catch: The only way you can achieve your potential is to first help your team achieve theirs."

Behind every great player is a coach who believed in that player more than the player believed in himself.

"So how do I help my team members achieve their potential?"

"That's where the system comes in," Coach said as he looked at his watch and shot a glance in the direction of his buddies playing pool. "But, unfortunately, it looks like our time for this evening is up."

"Are you serious?" Brad nearly screamed. "You're killing me! Can't you at least give me a hint?"

"Nope," Coach said with a smirk. "But here's what I want you to do. I want you to think about the three toughest challenges you're facing in getting your team to become more productive. Give it some thought, jot down some notes, and we'll reconvene next Friday. Same time, same place. Oh, and don't be late."

* * * * *

===

The only way you can achieve your potential is to first help your team achieve theirs.

===

The next day Brad returned from his morning jog, pulled a bottle of water from his refrigerator, and sat down on his leather couch to review his notes from the previous evening's coaching session. He took a yellow highlighter and began to mark some key phrases:

- *The secret is all in the approach. Stop acting like a manager and starting acting like a coach.*

- *The first step to becoming a frontline leader is to realize that the rules of the game have changed—and so too, must you.*

- *Great coaches consistently get the most out of their people because they consistently put the most into their people.*

- *Coaching is not merely something that you, as a manager, must do. A Coach is someone that you, as a leader, must become.*

- *As a coach, the more you give, the more you'll get. The more you care, the more they'll contribute.*

- *Behind every great player is a coach who believed in that player more than the player believed in himself.*

- *The only way you can achieve your potential is to first help your team achieve theirs.*

- *When all is said and done and we've completed this journey we call life, what will matter most is not we have achieved—but rather who we have become.*

Magic Pint Glass

The following Friday, Brad zipped into the lot at Halftime, parked his car in the first space he could find,
and jogged toward the front door.

It was 5:41 P.M. and he was late.

He looked to the back of the bar and saw Coach
sitting there—reading glasses on the tip of his nose—
drawing something on the back of a cocktail napkin.

Barely acknowledging the others in the bar, Brad
made a beeline back to Coach's corner, his apology
already prepared in his mind.

"Sales Manager, you're late," Coach grumbled,
beating Brad to the punch.

"I know, Coach. My bad. Today was the last day I could get fitted for my tux to get it back in time for next Friday's big awards shindig."

"Tux?" Coach raised an eyebrow. "You going to the Oscars or something? Have you written your acceptance speech yet?"

"No, but I have jotted down a few ideas," Brad said before realizing that Coach had been joking about the speech. "I mean," he continued, "I don't want to go up there looking like an idiot in front of 500 of the company's top brass, right? They might have second thoughts and take back the award!"

Coach just shook his head. "So did you do your homework?"

Brad nodded as he held up his journal.

"In case I forgot to mention it, the penalty for not showing up on time to one of my coaching sessions is a pint for every minute you're late," he said. "But since I'm in an especially good mood today because my Packers made the playoffs again, I'm going to give you a chance to get off the hook. I'll make you a bet. If I'm able to guess at least two out of the three biggest challenges you're having with improving the productivity of your team, then you buy the next round and we'll call it even. Anything less and it's on me."

"Wow!" Brad said. "A chance at free tuition? I'm in!"

Coach hunched over the table and started rubbing his pint glass as if it were some sort of magic crystal ball. "I see Es—three of them, in fact. The first problem has to do with a lack of Efficiency," he said. "It seems that most of your team is working hard, but unfortunately, they're working on the wrong things. They're so busy *reacting* instead of *acting* that they never actually get anything done."

"That's pretty darn impressive, old man."

Coach resumed his fortune teller position and rubbed his pint glass again. "The second E has to do Effort—or rather a lack of it. It seems that others on your team are coming into work and just going through the motions. It's as if you're only getting 150 horses out of a 350-horsepower engine. Right?"

"You're good! How'd you know that?" Brad asked.

"That's two for two," Coach said. "Do you want to go double or nothing and throw in a plate of nachos for good measure?"

"Bring it," Brad shot back. "But I guarantee you'll never get this one."

Coach rubbed his magic crystal pint for the third and final time. "Okay, it looks like the last E stands for . . . oh, yes . . . Effectiveness," he said. "Your salespeople may be making calls and taking meetings, but they're unsure of the next steps toward closing. As a result, they're getting lost in the sales process. Oh, and when it comes to getting them to input their data into the CRM system, forget about it. It's like trying to pull a pint of Guinness from an Irishman's hands!"

"Wrong!" the sales manager shouted.

Coach stared back in disbelief. "Really?" he said. "You're kiddin' me. What's the third one?"

Brad laughed. "Getting them to actually show up and have a pint with me so I don't have to sit up there celebrating all by myself, looking like a complete jackass!"

"I tell you what, kid," Coach said when he stopped laughing. "I'll cut you a break on the nachos. But while you're up, go ahead and get one for yourself, too."

As Brad left for the bar, Coach began scribbling on the chalkboard. He wrote,

$$\text{EMPLOYEE PRODUCTIVITY} = \text{EFFICIENCY} \times \text{EFFORT} \times \text{EFFECTIVENESS}$$

When Brad returned with their drinks, he stopped and stared at the chalkboard.

"Hey, wait a minute," he said as he placed the pints on the table. "I was told there'd be no math in this class. Did you forget? I'm a sales guy—not an engineer. The only numbers I pay attention to follow dollar signs."

"Okay, Mr. Sales Guy, do you want to learn how to solve the problems we were just talking about?" Coach said.

"Absolutely."

Coach drew a division line under the equation. Below it he wrote a question mark. "It's simple. Figure out the common denominator and you'll solve the problem."

The young manager just sat there quietly with a puzzled look on his face.

Sensing Brad's confusion, Coach glanced around the bar. When he found what he'd been searching for, he pointed to the wall behind one of the pool tables.

"Here's a hint," he said. "Go take a look at that picture over there next to the dart board—the one behind that pool table over there—and tell me what you see."

Brad walked over, stood about 10 feet in front of the picture, and slowly but loudly began to read, "We . . . proudly . . . serve . . . Strohs . . ."

Coach walked over to Brad and laughed. "No—take a closer look."

Brad walked a few steps closer.

"*Now* what do you see?" Coach asked.

Brad looked past the beer-marketing slogan and saw his reflection on the picture's mirrored surface.

"*Me*?" he said. "You think *I'm* the solution? Are you serious? Our senior management hasn't even figured out the magic formula, and you think *I* can do it?"

"I can guarantee you one thing: Your senior management has never tried what I'm about to teach you. You see, what they don't realize is that the fundamental problem is not a sales *skills* issue; it's a sales *leadership* issue. Or more specifically, a *frontline leadership* issue."

"I'm not sure I follow," said Brad as they headed back to Coach's corner.

"Think of it this way," said Coach as he slid into the booth. "You can draw up a beautiful game plan and have the best playbook, but if your quarterback on the field can't command the huddle, your team won't execute the plays."

As Brad took a seat across from him, Coach leaned forward and pointed at the young man's chest. "As a frontline manager, *you*, my friend, are like that quarterback on the field. *You* are the cornerstone of the team. You want to solve the problems we've been talking about and get your team to bring their A-game day in and day out? You want to learn how to become a coach and take *your* game and your team's performance to the next level?"

Brad nodded.

Coach flipped over the cocktail napkin. "Here's how you do it," he said.

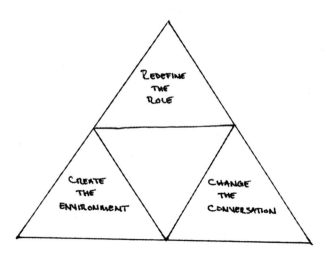

Mindset

Brad silently stared at the cocktail napkin as if it had some sort of mystical power. There it was in illustration form, scribbled on the back of a two-ply paper napkin with "Budweiser" stamped on the other side. He stared with anticipation. Surely it would stand on the table and begin speaking with the voice of James Earl Jones. Or perhaps sparks would fly from the edges as Coach levitated to some point just above the table. Or maybe a video would begin playing inside the napkin, like a message from Princess Leia to young Luke Skywalker.

A few seconds passed and the napkin didn't come to life. Brad looked up at Coach with a puzzled look as if to say, "Is *this* it? Really?"

"Listen, kid one thing you'll learn when you have as many gray hairs as I do is that the probability of a plan succeeding is in direct proportion to its simplicity. Don't get fancy. Keep it simple. It doesn't matter if we're talking about sales, marketing, customer service, operations, finance, IT, or HR. This system works. And a big part of the reason why it works is because it's simple to understand, easy to apply, and—most importantly—your team will absolutely love it."

Brad realized Coach had anticipated his reaction. Then he wondered if he had actually said out loud what he was thinking. Either way, Coach didn't seem to care. He was fired up and moving on.

"The weekly coaching conversation is by far the single most important skill you must master in order to get your team firing on all cylinders and consistently improving their level of performance." Coach paused for a moment before adding, "And since you're in sales, the objective of the weekly coaching conversation you're going to have with each member of your team will be to transform your one-on-ones from a contentious pipeline interrogation into a constructive coaching conversation."

"If you say so, Coach."

"However, before you're even ready to sit down with the people on your team and start having your weekly coaching conversations, there's some important prep work that needs to be done. So let's get to it. Are you ready?"

Brad gave an approving nod, and Coach launched into the plan, shifting his verbal motor into a higher gear.

"Step one: Redefine the Role.

"We touched on this earlier, but I want to reiterate a few key points," he said. "The difference that makes the difference is all in the approach. Stop acting like a manager; start acting like a coach. You need to redefine what you perceive your role to be. You must understand that, as a coach, you have one job and one job only: to pull every ounce of potential from each and every person on your team each and every day. Got it?"

As a coach you have one job and one job only: to pull every ounce of potential from each and every person on your team each and every day.

"Got it," the young manager said as he scribbled notes.

"They are your team and you are their coach," Coach continued. "What they may or may not be able to achieve is a direct reflection on you and your leadership abilities. No excuses. Their problems are your problems. Their victories are your victories. And their failures are your failures. Are you with me?"

Brad didn't even look up. He was still frantically taking notes, trying to capture every word Coach uttered.

"Yep."

"Good. Now write this down: How you define success will ultimately determine the level to which you succeed."

Brad slammed his pen down on the table and finally looked up. "Okay, now you've lost me."

"Let me show you what I mean." Coach grabbed a peanut and handed it to the young manager. "Here, see if you can throw this peanut into that garbage can right there."

Brad took the peanut and tossed it into the can a few feet away.

"Did you succeed?"

"Of course. I'm batting a thousand, aren't I?"

Coach handed him another peanut. "Give it another shot, but this time go for that garbage can way over there."

He pointed to a can about 20 feet across the room. Brad took aim as if he were shooting a three-pointer and tossed. The peanut came within a few inches of hitting a Stanford coed in the head before landing on the floor a few inches away from his target.

Coach said, "What about now? Are you still successful?"

"Come on," said the young manager. "Fifty percent might be good enough for some slackers, but it sure as heck isn't good enough for me."

Coach could tell by Brad's voice that he was joking, but was never one to let a coachable moment slip by.

"Interesting," he said to himself.

"What?"

"Interesting," Coach repeated.

"What!"

Coach turned his attention back to the young manager. "I just find it interesting that you're not satisfied with a 50 percent success rate throwing peanuts into a garbage can," he said. "Yet when only 50 percent of your team make their number, you want to celebrate because you're Sales Leader of the Year."

"Ouch," Brad said. "That's a low blow, Coach. But go ahead and bring it. I can take it."

Coach smiled. "Atta boy. Moving on, make a note: What you believe affects what they achieve."

"Come again?"

"What you do is controlled by how you think—your mindset." Coach explained. "And your mindset is basically just a series of beliefs and associations that control how you think and, ultimately, how you behave. For example, let's say one of your core beliefs is that winners are born—not made. In other words, what if you believed that trying to coach, develop, and improve your team's skill level and performance was a complete waste of time? How might this mindset affect your priorities—what you chose to focus on?"

After thinking for a moment, Brad replied, "I obviously wouldn't waste much time trying to coach them. I'd probably just focus on getting deals done and let HR worry about that."

"Exactly. Now just imagine for a moment if a professional coach had this same mindset. And after drafting a bunch of young college players, he sat them down and said, 'Gentlemen, I believe you either got it or you ain't got it. So me and the other coaches ain't gonna bother watching game film or trying to improve your performance, because we all know that's a complete waste of time.'"

Brad couldn't help but laugh out loud at how absurd this sounded.

"Seriously, what if a professional coach had this mindset?" Coach continued. "What if he believed that after draft day his job was more or less done, and all he needed to do was put them through training a few days a year and then show up for game day? How might this coach's mindset affect the likelihood that his players would reach their full potential? How might this coach's mindset impact the odds that his team could compete at the highest level?"

"Wow," said Brad, "I guess I'm really starting to see the connection between the approach of a sports coach and a frontline coach and how their roles are—or should be—very similar."

Coach nodded and launched into his next point.

"Make a note: Mind your mind. It all starts with you and your mindset. Change your mindset and you'll change your behavior. Change *your* behavior and you'll change *their* behavior. Change their behavior and you'll change their level of productivity. It's that simple. So before you waste all this time and energy trying to change your team's behavior, take a good long look in the mirror and first focus on changing yourself. As a leader, it all starts with you. *You* are the catalyst. Remember, nothing changes unless you do."

It all starts with you and your mindset. Change your mindset and you'll change your behavior. Change your behavior and you'll change their behavior. Change their behavior and you'll change their level of productivity.

The Talk

Little Nikki set a plate of nachos on the table in front of Coach and put a smaller, empty plate in front of Brad.

"Extra jalapenos, just like you like 'em, Coach," he said with a smile.

"Perfect! Thanks," Coach said as he slid the plate closer to Brad.

While Little Nikki returned to the bar, Brad stuffed his face and mumbled, "Step one, Redefine the Role. Stop acting like a manager and start acting like a coach. Got it. What's next?"

Coach passed the young manager a napkin and shook his head.

"Step two: Create the Environment. Or to put it another way," Coach said, "you've got to pull the weeds before you plant the seeds."

"Create what?" Brad said as he washed down a jalapeno with a swig of pilsner.

"Let me give you a quick example," Coach continued. "Early in Vince Lombardi's football coaching career, the bulk of his experience was as the head coach for a small, private high school—St. Cecilia's. While Lombardi was at St. Cecilia's, he won six straight parochial school state titles and at one point won 32 consecutive games. So when he finally landed a position in the pros as the offensive coordinator for the New York Giants, he figured he'd just use the same system—the same approach."

As an avid football fan, Brad knew all about Lombardi's legendary success as the head coach of the Green Bay Packers.

"Well, it obviously worked, right?" asked Brad. "I mean, he's one of the greatest coaches of all time."

"Nope," Coach said. "In fact, every time Lombardi tried to give his team some coaching, they tuned him out and wouldn't listen. In fact, they even mocked him for treating them like they were a bunch of high school kids. One day Lombardi had had enough. He decided to talk to Frank Gifford, the team leader and star quarterback at the time. After finding Frank in the locker room playing cards with a couple other team veterans, Lombardi approached them with complete humility and said, 'Guys—what the hell am I doing wrong?'

"And with that," Coach continued, "everything changed. You see, Lombardi learned a critical leadership lesson that day: To get your team to become coachable, *you* must first become coachable. To get your team to open up, *you* must first open up. To get your team to embrace developmental feedback, *you* must first embrace developmental feedback. As a coach, *you* set the standard for your team to follow. And your personal example is the most powerful leadership tool you have."

Brad did his best to capture all of Coach's insights in his journal. There was a pause in the conversation as Brad tapped his pen on the table and reviewed his notes.

*Pull the weeds before you
plant the seeds.*

"Setting an example makes a lot of sense," Brad said, "but what's that got to do with what you said a minute ago about pulling the weeds before you plant the seeds?"

Coach slapped the table and then reached for his pint.

"Every time I talk about Coach Lombardi, God rest his soul, I get all fired up," he said, washing down the last of the nachos on his plate. "Lombardi learned to plant seeds and help them grow. When we talk about the process of becoming a coach, what we're really talking about is planting seeds in the minds of your team—seeds of self-confidence, seeds of belief, desire, positive expectation, and, ultimately, seeds of greatness."

Coach paused to search for an analogy.

"A farmer hoping to reap a huge harvest," he continued, "wouldn't just walk up to any old dry, unfertile patch of dirt filled with weeds and start chucking out seeds like it's chicken feed, now would he?" To punctuate the point, Coach threw a handful of peanut shells across the floor.

To get your team to become coachable, you must first become coachable. To get your team to open up, you must first open up. To get your team to embrace developmental feedback, you must first embrace developmental feedback. As a coach, you set the standard for your team to follow. And your personal example is the most powerful leadership tool you have.

"Nope."

"Why not?"

"Because if you don't properly prepare the soil," Brad said, "the seeds won't take root. And if the field is already filled with weeds, the seeds will never stand a chance."

"Exactly," Coach said. "Make a note: Pull the weeds before you plant the seeds."

The young manager's journal again became the focus of his attention.

"Okay, here's what I mean," Coach added. "You need to hit the reset button on your relationship with your team. You need to sit down with each of them, *especially* your team leaders, and have a heart-to-heart with them to see where you stand. You need to identify and remove the friction points in your relationship that could be paralyzing your team's level of productivity. Just like Coach Lombardi, you've got to be the first one to put your cards on the table and ask, 'What am *I* doing wrong? What can *I* do better? How can *I* improve?'"

"Well, that's sure going to be a lot of fun," Brad sarcastically moaned.

"Just remember, when they start opening up and .telling you some things you'd probably rather not hear, don't get defensive. Don't judge—just listen. Really try to understand their perspective and see things through their eyes. Try to understand their perception of you and your leadership abilities, because you know what, Sales Manager?"

"What?"

"*Their* perception is *your* reality. Make a note: Leadership is a reciprocal process. In order for people to follow you, they must trust and believe in you. And in order for people to trust and believe in you, you must first trust and believe in them. Trust is the foundation of leadership and at the core of coaching."

Brad, still taking notes, didn't look up as he asked his next question. "Okay, so I sit down with each team member and ask what I'm doing wrong or, better yet, what I can improve on," he said. "And after they proceed to unload on me—telling me what a selfish jerk I've been—then what?"

"Simple," Coach said. "Apologize. But don't just say it; *mean* it. Look them in the eyes and tell them the truth. Be honest. Tell them exactly what you've shared with me over these past couple of weeks: that you've been selfish, that you've been doing it all and focusing only on your numbers instead of helping them reach *their* numbers. And then, most importantly, change your approach. Stop acting like a manager and start acting like a coach!"

Brad took a deep breath. "Okay," he said, "so once I've pulled all the weeds, then I start planting seeds, right?"

"Wrong."

"Wrong?"

"Dang, son, didn't your mama teach you anything about gardening? You can't treat different seeds all the same and expect them all to flourish, now can you? The next thing you've got to do is to figure out which types of seeds grow best under which conditions."

Coach pointed toward a line of old framed photos hanging on a nearby wall. Among the black-and-white mug shots of famous athletes and celebrities hung a picture of a racehorse, and Coach was pointing right at it.

"Ever see the movie *Seabiscuit?*" Coach asked.

"Great movie," Brad said. "One of my favorites. Right up there with *The Hangover* and *Caddy Shack*. I must have seen it a dozen times."

"Remember how, early on, Seabiscuit had a legendary trainer by the name of Fitzsimmons? If you'll recall, Fitzsimmons saw a lot of potential in Seabiscuit, but for some reason the horse just wasn't performing up to expectations. Fitzsimmons thought the horse was just too damn lazy. So do you remember what he did?"

"Yeah, he tried to break him down and beat it out him," Brad recalled.

"And did it work?" Coach asked.

"Nope," Brad said. "I think he either finished dead last or in the back of the pack in his first ten races."

"Right. So then along comes Seabiscuit's new trainer—an old, washed up horse-whisperer by the name of Tom Smith. And lo and behold, Seabiscuit starts winning every race, eventually becoming the number one racehorse in the entire country! Same horse. Same potential. But *vastly* different results."

Leadership is a reciprocal process. In order for people to follow you, they must trust and believe in you. And in order for people to trust and believe in you, you must first trust and believe in them.

Coach paused for a minute, letting his point sink in. "Let me ask you this: What made the difference? Was it the horse or the trainer?"

"The trainer," Brad answered without even thinking twice about it. "Seabiscuit had it in him the whole time."

"So what did Smith know that Fitzsimmons didn't?"

"Simple: He knew his horse."

"Exactly!" Coach said, his voice booming. "Make a note: Get to know your people. If you want them to trust you, you've got to earn it. You've got to make it a priority to continually invest in those relationships before they will start to pay dividends. Find out what is special and unique about each person on your team. Learn about their backgrounds, their upbringings, their styles, their idiosyncrasies, their strengths, their weaknesses, their hopes, dreams, and desires. Find out what drives them. Not only will this help you establish trust and rapport with your team, but it will also give you vital information that you're going to use during your weekly coaching conversations. This is how you'll inspire great performance from your team—just as Smith did with Seabiscuit. Are you following me?"

"Yep," Brad said as he finished jotting down his notes. "But I have a question. Going back to what you were talking about earlier, how will I know when it's time to start planting the seeds? At this point I don't think my team will even be receptive to what I have to say. When will I know I've developed enough trust and rapport so that they're open to having weekly coaching conversations?"

"Don't worry," said Coach. "You'll know. Trust your gut. You'll know."

The Greatest Gift

Coach returned with a second round of drinks and looked over Brad's notes as he settled back into his seat.

"You're catching on, Sales Manager," he said. "Had enough, or do you want more?"

Coach pulled out his own journal, wrote something down, and returned his gaze to his newest protégé.

"I'm ready for more," said Brad.

"Excellent!" said Coach, "because we're getting to the best part: the weekly coaching conversation."

"What's this weekly coaching conversation all about? I mean, obviously I'm still going to have to get forecast numbers and dig into the sales pipeline, but what else?" Brad asked.

Coach paused for several beats before replying.

"Let me ask you a question," Coach said. "What's the greatest gift you can give a salesperson?"

"A bluebird deal," Brad shot back without even thinking about it.

"Wrong."

"A great territory."

"Nope."

"A hot wife . . . a fancy car . . . I don't know!"

Coach laughed. "All right, all right," he said. "Let me help you out. The greatest gift you can give a salesperson—or any person for that matter—is confidence in themselves and their ability." He scooped a handful of peanuts from the bowl between them and continued. "As a salesperson, the first sales job is always on yourself. It doesn't matter how great your pitch is, how good your closing skills are, or how pretty that PowerPoint presentation might be—if the prospect can sense that you don't believe in yourself and what you're selling, she ain't gonna buy. It's that simple."

Coach continued. "In order to convince, *you* must first be convinced. You must have confidence in your product and your company. But most importantly, you must have confidence in yourself."

"Great stuff," Brad said as he wrote down more notes. "Great stuff."

"No need to kiss my a–," Coach said with a grin. "Remember how we talked about how it's your job to believe in your people more than they believe in themselves?"

Brad nodded.

"The next step is to transfer that belief—that sense of confidence and positive expectations—to your people. You must get *them* to raise their personal standards and believe that they are capable of achieving extraordinary things. You have to help them see that they haven't even scratched the surface of their potential."

Brad put his pen on the table and looked at Coach like a 170-pound wide receiver who had been asked to block a 370-pound defensive tackle.

"So how am I supposed to do *that*?" he asked.

Coach stared across the table deep in thought, as if he were diagramming a play in his head to send into the game.

"Let me ask you another question," Coach said. "Why do you think pro football coaches are so obsessed with watching game film?"

"Well, obviously, they watch game film to break down each player's individual performance," Brad answered. "To figure out what each person did right and what they did wrong so they can improve."

"Okay, and once the coaches have dissected their players' performance and pinpointed some things they need to work on in order to improve, what do they do with this information?" Coach asked. "Do they run up to HR asking for a performance evaluation sheet, write down what each team member needs to work on in order to improve, seal it up, and file it away until the end-of-year performance reviews?"

Brad laughed out loud at how absurd this sounded. "No, they use the info to give their players immediate feedback so they can improve next time."

"Feedback! Yes, lad, that's it! People need feedback to improve their performance, don't they? If your team doesn't know how they're doing—what they're doing right and what they're doing wrong—how can they adjust? How can they improve?"

Coach leaned forward. "Make a note: The only way to systematically improve individual performance is through consistently giving constructive coaching and developmental feedback. Just like in sports, there's a direct correlation between the *quantity* and the *quality* of coaching a person receives and his level of performance improvement."

"Quality and quantity of coaching equals performance improvement," Brad mumbled as he wrote.

"So let me ask you a question," Coach said. "How often are you giving your team constructive coaching and developmental feedback?"

Brad took a moment to think. "I don't know how 'constructive' or 'developmental' it is, but I guess once a year in their annual performance reviews."

Coach shook his head. "Once a year? You think coaching your team once a year is going to have *any* impact on trying to improve their performance?"

"Well, no," Brad said, "but isn't that pretty standard these days for most companies?"

Coach sighed. "Unfortunately, it is—which is why the vast majority of people are only performing at a fraction of their true potential. Think of it this way: If you have a *weekly* coaching conversation with each member of your team, you're giving them *50 times* more opportunities to improve their performance than the competition is getting. And it'll give you a consistent venue to look for those coachable moments."

Brad began writing. "Coachable moments?" he said.

"I've got another Packer story to illustrate my point," Coach said. "You love my Packer stories, don't you?"

"No, I'm actually a Cowboys fan."

Coach shook his head. "I won't hold it against you. Anyway, Jerry Kramer, one of the Packers' offensive linemen on Coach Lombardi's team, told a story about how he jumped offside once in a scrimmage. Lombardi immediately got in his face and yelled at the top of his lungs, 'The concentration period of a college student is 5 minutes, a high school student is 3 minutes, and a kindergartener is 30 seconds—and

The only way to systematically improve individual performance is to consistently give constructive coaching and developmental feedback.

you don't even have that! So where does that put you!'
After practice, Kramer went back into the locker room,
thinking, *There's not a chance in hell I'm ever going to
play for this guy again.* Then all of a sudden Lombardi bursts through the doors, heads straight over
to Kramer, bends down, looks him dead in the eye,
pats him on the back, and says, 'Son, one of these days
you're going to be the best damn guard in football.'
With that he turns and abruptly walks away. Kramer
later said that moment was the turning point in his
career. From that day on, he poured his heart out for
Coach Lombardi, because he knew that Lombardi believed in him and he didn't want to let him down. And
you know what?"

"What?"

"He didn't. Jerry Kramer became one of the
13 players on a 1-10-1 team that Lombardi inherited
back in '59 who either became an All Pro or Hall of
Fame player. You see, unlike most managers today,
Coach Lombardi didn't complain about the talent
that wasn't there—he focused on developing the talent that *was.*"

Coach again fixed his gaze on Brad. "Same player. Same team. Same potential. But *vastly* different results. So, what was the difference—the player or the coach?"

"The coach," Brad said without thinking twice about it.

"Exactly," Coach said. "Are you starting to understand how important your role is? Are you starting to understand that at the end of the day it's really *you* who makes the difference?"

"Yeah, I get it," said Brad.

Coach nodded. "Good. Never forget: What you say affects how they play."

What you say affects how they play.

The Weekly Coaching Conversation

Brad looked up from his journal, a puzzled expression on his face.

"I hear what you're saying about the importance of having a weekly coaching conversation, and I get that what I say affects how my team plays. But my question is, What *do* I say?"

Coach smiled. "Good question, kid. Let's start by looking at how you've been talking to your team and see how we might improve your game. What have you been telling them?"

"All I've been trained to do is grill my team on their sales pipelines and nag them about keeping their CRM system updated," Brad said.

"Well, we're here to fix that, aren't we? Now grab your pen and journal and get ready, because we're going to kick it up a notch. As you can see, the crew is getting restless back there."

Brad looked toward the pool tables, where a crowd of corporate executive types were partying like college kids, singing and dancing.

Coach jumped up, grabbed a piece of chalk, and starting scribbling something on the chalkboard behind the table. He wrote,

1. Shift the focus.

Coach put down the chalk and asked, "Why is it that most people come to work Monday morning with the best intentions to get a lot done, but at the end of the day have so little to show for their efforts?"

Brad shrugged. "I dunno."

"Let me give you a hint," Coach said. "Think back to the issue you said you were having about your team not working as *efficiently* as they should be."

From the look on Brad's face, he was drawing a blank.

Coach peered over the rim of his glasses and continued. "Still don't know? What if I told you that you were part of the problem?"

"Who me?" said Brad. "Not a chance! I'm the cocky guy who's got this management stuff all figured out. Remember?"

Coach smiled in recognition of his protégé's newfound sense of humility.

"Three important things you've got to keep in mind. First, as a sales manager—soon to be coach—one of the most important things you can do to improve your team's productivity is to figure out a system to help align their daily focus toward critical pipeline development activities. Second, you need to stop focusing so much on the prize that you forget about the process. And finally, you've got to understand that what gets reinforced, gets done. Focus controls behavior. Questions control focus. If, as a frontline manager, you are not *knowingly* asking the right questions, you are *unknowingly* reinforcing the wrong behaviors."

*Stop focusing so much on the prize
that you forget about the process.*

"Whew!" Brad said, wiping his brow. "Where'd you learn all this stuff? You sure as heck didn't pick it up on the football field."

"No, I learned most of it while studying sports psychology," Coach said, "but that's beside the point. Anyhow, when you sit down with your team for your weekly one-on-ones, what type of questions are you asking?"

Brad half-jokingly replied, "I'm all about *Glengary Glen Ross*. A-B-C: *Always. Be. Closing.* So of course I ask the same two questions that every other sales manager asks: One, how big's the deal? And two, when is it closing?"

Coach shook his head and sighed. "Well that explains it."

"Explains what?"

"Why you can't get your salespeople to prospect."

Coach grabbed another cocktail napkin and drew a sales funnel diagram on the back. At the top he wrote "all sales prospects" and at the bottom he wrote "final sales."

Coach tapped on the drawing with his pen and said, "When you ask those questions—'How big is the deal?' and 'When is it closing?'—where on the sales funnel does that put the focus?"

PRINCIPLE: WHAT GETS REINFORCED, GETS DONE

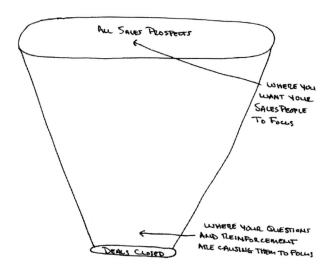

ALL SALES PROSPECTS

WHERE YOU WANT YOUR SALESPEOPLE TO FOCUS

WHERE YOUR QUESTIONS AND REINFORCEMENT ARE CAUSING THEM TO FOCUS

DEALS CLOSED

"On the bottom."

"And to get them to start doing more prospecting on a more consistent basis," Coach continued, "where on the sales funnel *should* you be focusing their attention?"

"On the top."

"Are you starting to see the problem here?"

"I never realized how much of an impact what *I* say affects what *they* do."

Coach just smiled. "Remember: A skilled coach uses questions to control focus and direct behavior to improve performance."

When Brad finished writing his notes, Coach wrote the second key point on the chalkboard:

2. Don't just celebrate the touchdowns— celebrate the first downs.

"Remember how you said your team just wasn't putting forth the effort? You said they seemed to be just going through the motions—doing just enough to skate by. What if I told you that you were part of this problem, as well?"

Brad frowned. "Hey, wait a minute. I'm starting to see a theme here. What the hell is this? Beat-up-on-Brad day?"

Coach smiled. "Relax. While you may be part of the problem, you're going to be an even bigger part of the solution. Just do what I say and you'll be a hero."

Don't just celebrate the touchdowns—celebrate the first downs.

"So what does my team's lackluster performance have to do with first downs?" Brad asked.

"Make a note," Coach said. "Long-term success requires short-term focus. And the fastest way to improve performance is to help your team set daily and weekly process-oriented goals and then positively reinforce small, incremental improvements. This is not some management gimmick; it's a scientific fact," said Coach. "What gets reinforced gets done. Whether we're talking about succeeding in business, sports, teaching, or parenting, the same principles apply. The goal here is steady, consistent progress—day in and day out. All you're trying to do is to get them to be a little bit better today than they were yesterday."

Coach wrote the third and final point on the board:

3. Embrace mistakes as coachable moments.

"This one has to do with some of the challenges your team is having around *effectiveness*—their skill competency level."

What gets reinforced, gets done.

"Wait a minute," Brad interrupted. "Let me guess. This one's my fault, too."

"Actually, no," Coach said. "Chalk this one up to conventional wisdom not being all that wise. For some reason the conventional wisdom has always been that it was the primary responsibility of HR, enablement, or outside trainers to coach, train, and develop *your* team. It's not. That's *your* job. In fact, that's the single most important aspect of your job and why redefining your role—from being a manager to being a coach—is so critical."

"The only way your team members can hone their skills and consistently improve their performance is if you are actively coaching and reinforcing their skill development on a *weekly* basis. That's why the weekly coaching conversation is so important. And frankly, without this critical management reinforcement piece of the puzzle in place, trying to train frontline employees is a colossal waste of time, energy, and money, because it won't stick."

Brad continued taking notes while Coach took a sip from his pint.

Embrace mistakes as coachable moments.

"Building a highly productive team can only be achieved through the identification and perfection of seemingly small things consistently done right over time. But here's the deal: We learn far more from our mistakes than we do from our successes," Coach said. "If you only give your team positive reinforcement, they may feel all warm and fuzzy, but they're never going to improve. So as you're evaluating your team's performance and giving them positive reinforcement, it's also important to take note of their mistakes as well.

"Keep in mind that the objective here is not to *criticize*; it's to *coach*," Coach added. "Learn to embrace mistakes as coachable moments. As long as you've done a good job of establishing trust, rapport, and shared interest with your team, they'll understand that your intent is to help them, not hurt them. If your people feel that you genuinely have their best interests in mind, they'll embrace your feedback and act on it."

The buzzing of a cell phone interrupted Coach before he could move to another point. He pulled the phone from his pocket and looked at the number on the screen.

"Gimme a sec. I need to take this call," he said as he stepped away from the table.

"Everything okay?" Brad asked when Coach returned a few minutes later.

"I hate to do this, but I've got to cut this session a little short. I have to catch the next flight out to Europe for an emergency board meeting."

Brad had begun to see Coach as larger than life, but a spur-of-the-moment business trip to Europe still stunned him a bit.

"Really?" he said.

"Yeah, one of the companies I'm an active board member for is trying to close an M&A deal they've been working on for quite a while. I'll probably be gone for a couple of weeks."

Brad noticed that Coach's tone was casual, as if the trip were routine as a drive around the block.

"I'm sorry I won't be here next Friday to celebrate after you receive that award," Coach said.

"No worries," said Brad, doing his best to mask his disappointment.

Coach slapped Brad on the back with his left hand and extended an envelope in his right hand. "I got you a little something," he said. "But don't open it until right before the awards banquet."

Brad flipped the envelope over a few times, resisting the temptation to slice it open and examine what was inside. As Coach made his way toward the exit, yelling mildly obscene good-byes to his crew, Brad stuck the envelope in his journal and put them both in his jacket pocket.

"Safe travels, Coach," he yelled across the room.

The Leadership Moment

Brad pushed hard through the traffic on Highway 101 as he made his way toward the Imperial Hotel in downtown San Francisco for the NPC annual awards banquet. The big day had finally arrived. Five hundred of the company's top executives were gathered in the ballroom of one of the swankiest hotels in the city—and it looked for all the world like the winner of the event's biggest award would arrive late.

"The Sales Leader of the Year ought to buy himself one of these stupid monkey suits," Brad said to himself as he exited the highway and sat anxiously waiting for the light to change.

The tux had put him behind schedule. The formal wear store had sent the wrong suit over, and Brad quickly decided he'd rather arrive late than dress in teal and look like a 1970s lounge singer. By the time he took it back, got the right tux, changed, and drove to the hotel, he had already missed the salads and the main course was being served.

The people on Brad's team—who'd been invited to attend so they could witness him receiving the award—were seated at a table near the back of the room. Brad noticed them from across the room as soon as he walked in. He gave them a quick nod and a wave as he hurriedly made his way toward a table at the front. They obligingly returned the wave and went back to buttering their rolls.

Brad took his seat, apologizing to his tablemates for his tardiness. Suddenly, it hit him: In his rush to fix the tux fiasco, he'd forgotten to open the envelope Coach had given him before he left. He pulled his journal from his jacket pocket, slid out the envelope, and opened it. Inside, he found a handwritten, heart-felt congratulatory note from Coach.

"Aren't you going to eat, Brad?" asked Janet Gomez, the senior vice president of operations for NPC.

Her question startled Brad, who'd been lost in thought.

"What's that?" he said, looking up from the note. "Oh, no. I had a late lunch. I'm not real hungry."

He downed the glass of iced tea in front of him, trying to bring life to his dry throat. He made a feeble attempt to join in the group's conversation to hide the fact that his stomach was doing flip-flops. As the awards ceremony began, Brad sat with his palms sweating, his heart racing, and his mind drifting back to the conversations he'd had with Coach over the past few weeks at Halftime. His mind was in a fog when he heard the applause and realized it had followed his name flowing off the lips of NPC's CEO, Martin Cower.

"And for the final award of the evening, it brings me great pleasure to introduce our Sales Leader of the Year . . . Brad Hutchinson!" Cower announced.

Adrenaline pumping and with his speech in hand, Brad slowly walked to the podium. As the applause finally died down, Brad looked across the now silent room filled with a who's who of his company's power players, all dressed to the nines. Suddenly it was as if the scene had switched into slow motion. He could hear his heart beating and the quickening of his breath. His sweating palms tightly clutched the speech he had labored over.

Brad looked down at his speech notes. *I can't do this,* he thought as he reviewed the notes one last time. *This just isn't me anymore.* With a fresh wave of courage and inspiration, he took a deep breath and began, "A wise man once told me . . ."

Abruptly, Brad stopped. His voice had cracked. He cleared his throat and started again, this time a little louder into the microphone.

"A wise man once told me to get it out of my head and into my heart," he said. "So here goes—"

With that, he crinkled up the speech and tossed it over his shoulder, drawing light laughter from the crowd.

"When I was first promoted into management," he said, "I thought I had all the answers. Now I realize that's not my job. My job is to ask all the right questions. When I first became a manager, I thought

my job was to make *my* number. I was wrong. I now realize my job is to help my *team* make *their* numbers. When I first became a manager, I thought it was all about me. I was wrong. I now realize it's about *them*—my team."

Brad pointed to the table at the back of the room where his team was sitting and called out each person by name.

"I now realize it's about helping my team achieve *their* dreams, *their* goals, and *their* aspirations. It's about helping them grow and improve so that they can achieve their potential—as professionals and as human beings."

Brad took another breath but his pause was brief.

"And while the scoreboard may indicate that I've succeeded as a sales manager," he said, "the truth is . . . I now realize that I've failed as a sales leader. I've learned a lot over the past few weeks. I now realize that I've been wrong about a lot of things. But there's one thing I know I'm right about—and that's that I am not worthy of this award. You see, I'd gladly accept it if it weren't for one word: It doesn't say sales *manager*;

it says sales *leader*. So as much as I sincerely appreciate the acknowledgement, I'm afraid I must respectfully decline the award."

A wave of shock rolled over the audience, beginning with the look on CEO Martin Cower's face and working its way to the back of the room where Brad's team sat in stunned silence. A murmur of whispers quickly filled the ballroom as the people at each table began wondering out loud: "Is this really happening?"

With Coach's note still fresh in his mind, Brad added one final thought.

"A wise man once told me that when all is said and done and we've finally completed this journey we call life, what will matter most is not what we have achieved—but rather who we have become," Brad said with renewed confidence. "And while I realize I have a long way to go toward reaching my potential both as a person and as a leader"—he paused, overcome with emotion as he realized he'd seized his leadership moment—"I think I'm finally at least reading from the right playbook."

With that, Brad turned from the podium, stepped off the stage, and walked through the center of the crowd toward the back doors. A few sporadic claps finally broke the awkward silence, then quickly grew into a roaring applause, and, by the time he reached the exit, a standing ovation.

Stepping into the cool Bay Area evening, Brad thought to himself, *Great—now what?* After considering his options, he smiled and said, "What else?"

* * * * *

An hour or so later Brad walked into Halftime. It was a typical Friday evening crowd. He parked himself at the bar, ordered a pint, and began chatting with Little Nikki and a few regulars he'd gotten to know over the past few weeks. The familiar surroundings helped him sense Coach's presence, but he couldn't help wondering what the old man was doing at that particular moment in Europe.

After finishing his first pint, Brad excused himself from the small talk and made his way to the restroom.

He stood over the old tin horse trough, perusing last week's sports section pinned to the corkboard in front of him. Without warning, the door behind him flew open and crashed against the wall.

"Now that's a *real* fancy suit you got on there!" bellowed a loud, familiar voice. "Don't you think you're a little overdressed for a sh—hole like this? What, you just come from a funeral or somethin'?" Coach's raucous laughter filled the room.

Brad just about fell over. "What are *you* doing here?" he shouted. "I thought you were still in Europe!"

"Just got back a couple of hours ago," Coach said. "We ended up getting the deal done sooner than expected, so I decided to cut the trip a little short. I probably would've made it in time for your big award if it hadn't been for a weather delay in Chicago."

Coach paused and looked at his newest protégé. "So how did it go, kid?"

Brad desperately wanted to unload all the details about how he had "seized the moment" and declined the award, because he knew how proud Coach would be of him. But for some reason, it just didn't feel right.

"It was uneventful," he said. "You know how boring those stupid things are."

With a twinkle in his eye and a knowing smile on his face, Coach put his hand on Brad's shoulder as they walked out of the restroom. He pointed back to the pool tables, where a large group of Coach's crew had gathered.

"Come on, kid, why don't you come on over and join us?"

As he started toward the pool tables, Coach noticed something out of the corner of his eye. A group of about ten young professionals all dressed to the hilt had just walked into the bar and were standing in the entrance scanning the place as if they were looking for someone in particular.

"On second thought, Sales Leader," Coach said as he patted Brad on the back and directed his attention toward the front door, "it looks like some friends came to help you celebrate after all."

Closing Thoughts

How to improve employee performance and transform organizational productivity

Building an organization to succeed in the marketplace is like leading a football team to victory on the field. There are owners or shareholders, executives who set goals, manage budgets, and handle administrative duties. In both cases, there's a team, a strategic game plan, and a tactical playbook. But when it comes down to it, there is one key player who the entire game plan is dependent upon—the quarterback. And that position exists in the corporate world as well; we call them the frontline manager.

When a frontline manager can't "command the huddle," as Coach likes to say in the fable, the results manifest themselves in a number of ways:

- Inconsistent, suboptimal frontline employee performance

- Low morale, difficulty attracting top talent and retaining top performers

- Stalled strategic change initiatives due to a lack of bottom-up buy-in

- Wasted time, energy, and budget on training initiatives that fail to stick

- Organizational productivity that is virtually paralyzed

All of the preceding issues are symptomatic of the same fundamental problem: the frontline managers' inability to successfully coach, develop, and lead their teams.

Research shows that, despite their critical roles, frontline managers have not been given the tools they need to lead their teams

---

Given the critical role that frontline managers play in an organization's success, a recent McKinsey study[1] corroborated our own research findings, in that:

- Nearly 70 percent of senior executives are not satisfied with the performance of their frontline managers, while 81 percent of frontline managers themselves are not satisfied with their own performance.

- Only 10 percent of companies believe their frontline managers are prepared to successfully coach, develop, and lead their teams.

[1] De Smet, A., McGurk, M., and Vinson, M. 2010. McKinsey Survey Results: How Companies Manage the Front Line Today. New York: McKinsey & Company.

- Frontline managers receive the least amount of training and development (9 percent) while frontline employees receive the most (27 percent).

Employee performance is directly tied to the quantity and the quality of coaching they receive

---

The foundation of transforming organizational productivity is improving individual performance. The only way to systematically improve individual performance is to provide constructive coaching and developmental feedback. In fact, countless studies have shown that there's a direct correlation between the quantity and the quality of constructive coaching an individual receives and his or her level of performance improvement.

Question: How much constructive coaching and developmental feedback are your frontline employees currently receiving?

The truth is, relying on quarterly performance reviews is not nearly enough to move the needle. And, as you probably already realize, relying on annual training events is not enough to get the job done. Coaching and developing people to consistently improve their performance is not an event. It's an ongoing process that should be inextricably tied to everything managers do on a *weekly* basis.

Without a doubt, teaching frontline managers how to facilitate a Weekly Coaching Conversation is the single most important skill they must master in order to systematically improve their team's performance and your organization's productivity.

Acknowledgments

This book has been many years in the making and would not have been possible without the incredible group of people I have been so blessed to call my team.

First and foremost my heartfelt thanks and gratitude go to

- *my amazing wife, Claudia, for being my best friend since the day we met and for all her patience and support over the years. You are truly one in a million.*

- *my two beautiful girls, Grace and Giselle, for bringing so much joy and love into our lives.*

- *my parents, Larry and Sandy, for blessing me with the most amazing childhood one could hope for and for being the best "Bama" and "Peepa" in the world. You are amazing.*

- *my siblings, Kevin, Jeff, and Ashley, for always being there. I'm so grateful our relationship has evolved and that we've been able to become such great friends over the years.*

- *my in-laws, George and Gudrun, for all of the love and support you've given us over the years. We would not be where we are without you.*

I would also like to sincerely thank my world-class team, including

- *my agent and friend, Kevin Small, for his genius and generosity. Without you and all your help and guidance, this would all still be a dream.*

- *my publisher, Karen Kreiger and the Evolve team, who believed in me and this book from the very first day. You are a joy to work with and the best publishing partner an author could hope for.*

- *Stephen Caldwell, whose help early on was instrumental in bringing this fable to life.*

- *Martha Lawrence, whose masterful touch took the manuscript to the next level. You are truly a master of the trade.*

- *Bonnie Vandewater for always being there at the last minute to edit and proofread my writing.*
- *Bill Chiaravalle and his artistic touch on the beautiful design of this book.*
- *All of my coaches over the years—especially Bill Strauss, Ken Blanchard, and Stephen Covey—for passing along your wisdom and example.*
- *Father Nick for feeding my soul every Sunday at St. Therese of Carmel and for inspiring me to use my God-given gifts to make a positive difference in people's lives.*

Without each and every one of you and all your help and support, I would not be able to achieve my dream of sharing this message with the world. And so for this, I owe you a deep debt of gratitude.

About the Author

Brian Souza is founder and president of ProductivityDrivers, an innovative corporate training company specializing in improving employee performance and organizational productivity. As a respected thought leader in leadership development, organizational  productivity, and sales, he works with leading companies worldwide as a keynote speaker and management consultant. He is also the author of the critically acclaimed book *Become Who You Were Born to Be* (Random House, 2007), which has been published in multiple languages around the world.

Brian lives in San Diego with his wife, Claudia, their two daughters, Grace and Giselle, their cat, Mieze, and their dog, Gunnar.

To learn more, please visit www.BrianSouza.com

FIND ME on  FOLLOW ME on